FLOWCHART
AND
ALGORITHM BASICS

FLOWCHART
AND
ALGORITHM BASICS

The Art of Programming

A. B. CHAUDHURI

MERCURY LEARNING AND INFORMATION
Dulles, Virginia
Boston, Massachusetts
New Delhi

Publisher: David Pallai
MERCURY LEARNING AND INFORMATION
22841 Quicksilver Drive
Dulles, VA 20166
info@merclearning.com
www.merclearning.com
1-800-232-0223

A.B. Chaudhuri. *Flowchart and Algorithm Basics: The Art of Programming.*
ISBN: 978-1-68392-537-8

Library of Congress Control Number: 2020938815

202122321   Printed on acid-free paper in the United States of America.

CONTENTS

PREFACE

The inspiration for this book came from my students, who asked that I write such a book so that others can grasp the art of programming logic development easily and quickly. This book is aimed at inculcating problem-solving skills in beginners in computing science who might be ill-prepared to handle the problem-solving aspects of the discipline.

Although no book can be claimed to be self-contained, an attempt has been made to equip the readers with all the best, most efficient, and well-structured programming logic in the form of flowcharts and algorithms. The illustrative examples will definitely encourage and enable students to solve the problems in the exercises (and they will enjoy the task). As the task of logic development is an art, the same problem can be solved in a number of ways. Self-starters may try different logical approaches to the solutions or instructors may guide the readers to redevelop the solutions using different approaches.

Suggestions for improvement of this work are greatly appreciated.

A. B. Chaudhuri
May 2020

CHAPTER 1

INTRODUCTION TO PROGRAMMING

INTRODUCTION

A computer program is a sequential set of instructions written in a computer language that is used to direct the computer to perform a specific task of computation.

Observe that the definition demands that any set of instructions must be such that the tasks will usually be performed sequentially unless directed otherwise. Each instruction in the set will express a unit of work that a computer language can support. In general, high level languages, also known as 3GLs, support one human activity at a time. For example, if a computational task involves the determination of the average of three numbers, then it will require at least three human activities, *viz.*, getting the numbers, obtaining the sum of the numbers, and then obtaining the average. The process will therefore require three instructions in a computer language. However, it can be done using two instructions, also: first by obtaining the numbers and second by obtaining the sum and the average.

The objective of programming is to solve problems using computers quickly and accurately.

FLOWCHARTING AND ALGORITHMS

A problem is something the result of which is not readily available. A set of steps involving arithmetic computation and/or logical manipulation is required to obtain the desired result. There is a law called the *law of equifinality* that states that the same goal can be achieved through different courses of action and a variety of paths, so the same result can be derived in a number of ways. For example, consider the task of sending a message to one of your friends. There are many ways in which this can be done. First, you can convey the message over the phone if your friend possesses a phone. Second, you can send it by post. Third, you can send it through a courier service. If the message is urgent, then you can try to use the quickest means for sending it. If it is not urgent, then you will choose to send it in the least expensive but most reliable way of doing it. Depending upon the urgency, you will decide the most effective way of doing it. This most effective way is called the *optimum way*. The different ways of solving a problem are called *solution strategies*. The optimum way of solving a problem to get the desired result can be achieved by analyzing different strategies for the solution and then selecting the way that can yield the result in the least time using the minimum amount of resources. The selection process will depend on the efficiency of the person and his/her understanding of the problem. He/she must also be familiar with different problem-solving techniques. Determining the set of steps required to solve a given problem is an art. It shows how well a person can arrange a set of steps so that others can follow it. A type of analysis called *task analysis* is required to reach the solution from a problem definition that states what is to be achieved.

A set of steps that generates a finite sequence of elementary computational operations leading to the solution of a given problem is called an *algorithm*. An algorithm may be too verbose to follow. The textual description of an algorithm may not be understood quickly and easily. This is why a pictorial representation may be used as a substitute for an algorithm. Such a pictorial representation is called a *flowchart*. Formally speaking, a flowchart is a diagrammatic representation of the steps of an algorithm. In a flowchart, boxes of different shapes are used to denote different types of operations. These boxes are then connected by lines with arrows denoting the flow or direction to which one should proceed to know the next step. The connecting lines are known as *flow lines*. Flowcharts may be classified into two categories:

(i) Program Flowchart   **(ii)** System Flowchart

Program flowcharts act like mirrors of computer programs in terms of flowcharting symbols. They contain the steps of solving a problem unit for a specific result.

System flowcharts contain the solutions of many problem units together that are closely related to each other and interact with each other to achieve a goal. We will first focus on program flowcharts.

A *program flowchart* is an extremely useful tool in program development. First, any error or omission can be more easily detected from a program flowchart than it can be from a program because a program flowchart is a pictorial representation of the logic of a program. Second, a program flowchart can be followed easily and quickly. Third, it serves as a type of documentation, which may be of great help if the need for program modification arises in future.

The following five rules should be followed while creating program flowcharts.

- Only the standard symbols should be used in program flowcharts.
- The program logic should depict the flow from top to bottom and from left to right.
- Each symbol used in a program flowchart should contain only one entry point and one exit point, with the exception of the decision symbol. This is known as the *single rule*.
- The operations shown within a symbol of a program flowchart should be expressed independently of any particular programming language.
- All decision branches should be well-labeled.

The following are the standard symbols used in program flowcharts:

Terminal: used to show the beginning and end of a set of computer-related processes

Input/Output: used to show any input/output operation

Computer processing: used to show any processing performed by a computer system

Predefined processing: used to indicate any process not specially defined in the flowchart

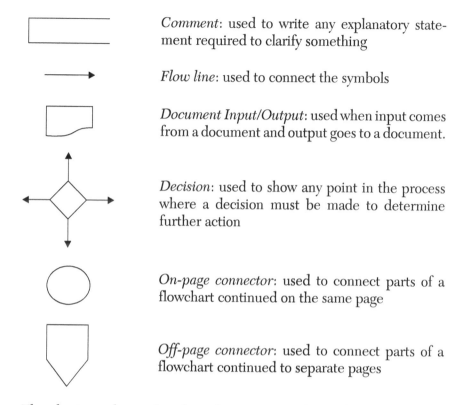

Comment: used to write any explanatory statement required to clarify something

Flow line: used to connect the symbols

Document Input/Output: used when input comes from a document and output goes to a document.

Decision: used to show any point in the process where a decision must be made to determine further action

On-page connector: used to connect parts of a flowchart continued on the same page

Off-page connector: used to connect parts of a flowchart continued to separate pages

Flowcharts can be used to show the sequence of steps for doing any job. A set of simple operations involving accepting inputs, performing arithmetic operation on the inputs, and showing them to the users demonstrate the *sequence logic structure* of a program. The following flowchart shows the steps in cooking rice and then utilizing the cooked rice.

The algorithm for the flowchart about cooking rice is as follows:

Step 1. Take the rice to be cooked.
Step 2. Procure the container.
Step 3. Procure the water.
Step 4. Wash the rice in the water.
Step 5. Put the rice into the container.
Step 6. Pour water into the container.
Step 7. IF WATER LEVEL = 1 INCH ABOVE THE RICE
    THEN GOTO STEP 8
    ELSE GOTO STEP 6
ENDIF

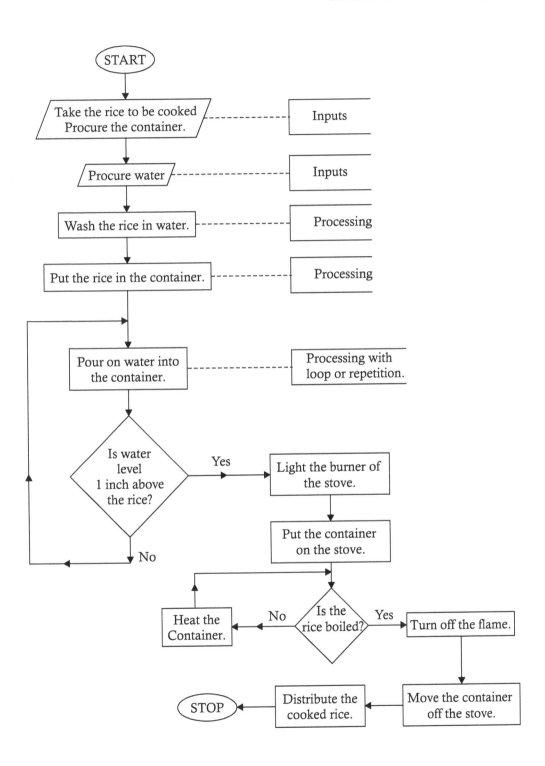

Step 8. Light the burner on the stove.

Step 9. IF THE RICE IS BOILED
   THEN GOTO STEP 12
   ELSE GOTO STEP 10
   ENDIF

Step 10. Heat the container.

Step 11. Go to step 9.

Step 12. Turn off the flame.

Step 13. Move the container off the stove.

Step 14. Distribute the cooked rice.

Step 15. STOP.

The main purpose of flowcharting is to discover/invent the sequence of steps for showing the solution of a problem through arithmetic and/or logical manipulations for which we can instruct computers. The problems for flowcharting and algorithm development that we will consider here are based primarily on computational procedures.

We now consider different problem definitions, followed by the task analysis, and then the desired flowchart. We denote the assignment operation using an arrow sign. The direction of the arrow implies the destination of the assignment. For example, "A ← B" means that the value contained in B is assigned to A. This, however, does not mean that the value of B is lost in A; it implies that the value contained in B is copied into A so that A and B contain the same thing. We use the symbol * or x to indicate a multiplication operation.

Let us consider a problem, the goal of which is to construct a flowchart to show the procedure to obtain the sum of two given numbers.

This is a very simple task. To solve the problem, we require two numbers as inputs. The numbers can then be added together to derive the sum. Observe that as a user of the procedure, you can provide any two numbers. As we wish to construct a procedure, we should not specify any arbitrary pair of numbers for the procedure. It is more convenient if we denote the input values symbolically. Symbols represent the given numbers. A similar symbol can be used to represent the sum. Another concept used during programming is that of *containers* called *variables*. The symbols for representing input data values or the output results may be treated as the containers of the values' input or output. Whatever they are, the data values are the contents of the variables. Variables are symbolic representations of containers for holding data or information. We follow the convention that a single word consisting of one to any number of characters can be used as the name of a variable. A *variable* is actually a named collection of one or more memory locations of a computer treated as a single container. Its content may vary depending on a user's operation. The following discussion explains the following flowchart of the desired procedure.

The program logic structure illustrated in the flowcharts of this chapter is the sequence logic structure.

Problem 1.1. *Draw a flowchart to show how the sum of two numbers can be obtained.*

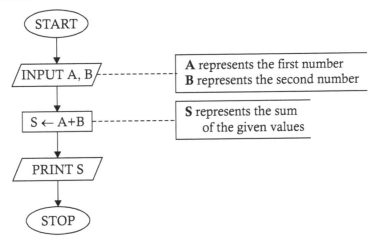

The following algorithm shows the desired procedure:

Step 1. INPUT TO A, B
Step 2. S ← A+B
 (Store the sum of the values in A and B in S)
Step 3. PRINT S
 (Show the sum obtained in Step 2)
Step 4. STOP

A sequence structure shows simple input, output, and process operations.

Problem 1.2. *Construct a flowchart to show the procedure for obtaining the average of two given numbers.*

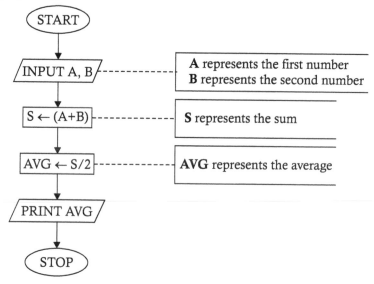

Task Analysis. From the concept of determining the average of two given numbers, we know that the given numbers must be added together to obtain the sum first; the sum is then divided by 2 to obtain the average. The flowchart for Problem 1.2 illustrates this idea.

The algorithm corresponding to Problem 1.2 is shown below:

Step 1. INPUT TO A, B
Step 2. S ← A + B
(Store the sum of the values in A and B and store in S)
Step 3. AVG ← S/2
(Compute the average)
Step 4. PRINT AVG (Show the average)
Step 5. STOP

Problem 1.3. *Construct a flowchart to show how to obtain the volume of a rectangular box.*

Task Analysis. We know that the formula to determine the volume of a rectangular box is Volume = Length × Breadth × Height. To determine the volume of a rectangular box, we need to know the length, breadth, and height of the box. When these values are multiplied together, the product represents the desired volume.

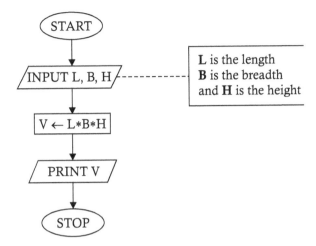

The algorithm for the solution of Problem 1.3 is given below:

Step 1. INPUT TO L, B, H
Step 2. COMPUTE V ← L*B*H
Step 3. PRINT V
Step 4. STOP

Problem 1.4. *Construct a flowchart to show how to obtain the daily wage of a worker on the basis of the hours worked during the day.*

Task Analysis. The daily wage depends on two factors: the hours worked and hourly rate of pay. When the hours worked is multiplied by the rate of pay, the product represents the wage of the worker.

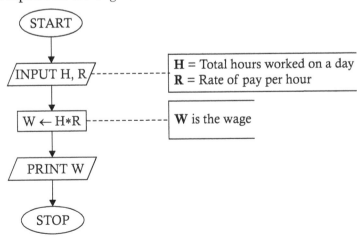

The algorithm for the solution of Problem 1.4. is given below:

Step 1. INPUT TO H, R
Step 2. COMPUTE W ← H*R
(Store the product of the values in H and R in W)
Step 3. PRINT W
Step 4. STOP

Problem 1.5. *Construct a flowchart to show how to obtain the area of a triangle on the basis of the base and height.*

Task Analysis. We know that the formula to find out the area of a triangle is

$$\text{Area} = \frac{1}{2} \times \text{base} \times \text{height}$$

The inputs required to obtain the area of a triangle are its base and height. We can then put the values in the above formula to obtain the area.

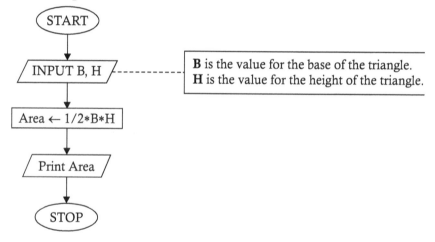

The algorithm corresponding to the above procedure is given below:

Step 1. INPUT TO B, H
(B is for the base and H is for the height of the triangle)

Step 2. COMPUTE AREA ← $\frac{1}{2}$*B*H

Step 3. PRINT AREA
Step 4. STOP

Problem 1.6. *Develop a flowchart to show the steps in finding the simple interest on a given amount at a given rate of interest.*

Task Analysis. We know that if P is the principal, R is the rate of interest, and T is the term in years, then the simple interest I is given by the formula $I = \dfrac{P*R*T}{100}$. To determine the simple interest on a given amount, we need the principal amount (P), the rate of interest (R), and the term in years (T). By putting the values in the formula above, we get the desired simple interest.

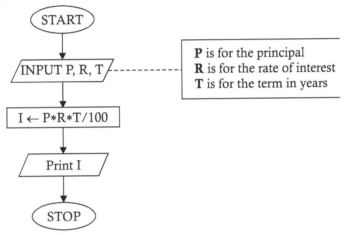

The algorithm corresponding to the above logic is given below:

Step 1. INPUT TO P, R, T
Step 2. COMPUTE I ← P*R*T / 100
Step 3. PRINT I
Step 4. STOP

Problem 1.7. *If P amount of money is invested for N years at an annual rate of interest I, the money grows to an amount T, where T is given by $T = P(1 + I/100)^N$. Draw a flowchart to show how T is determined.*

Task Analysis. The solution to this problem is very simple, and it is similar to the preceding one. The inputs required are the values for P, I, and N. The output T can then be obtained by putting the values in the formula.

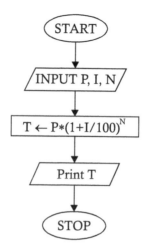

The algorithm corresponding to Problem 1.7 is given below:

Step 1. INPUT TO P, I, N

Step 2. COMPUTE $T \leftarrow P * \left(1 + \dfrac{I}{100}\right)^N$

Step 3. PRINT T
Step 4. STOP

Problem 1.8. *Construct a flowchart to show how a student's registration number and grades in 3 subjects, m_1, m_2, and m_3, are displayed along with the total average grade.*

Task Analysis. The data supplied as inputs are the registration number and *grades* obtained in three subjects. The registration number contributes nothing to the process of deriving the desired output; it just identifies the person about whom the total grade and the average grade are obtained. The total grade can be obtained by taking the sum of the marks m_1, m_2, and m_3, and the average can be obtained by dividing the total by 3. The steps are illustrated below.

The algorithm corresponding to the above problem is given below:

Step 1. INPUT TO REGN-NO
Step 2. INPUT TO M1, M2, M3
  (M1, M2, and M3 are for holding the grades in three subjects)
Step 3. COMPUTE T ← M1 + M2 + M3
Step 4. COMPUTE AVG ← T/3
Step 5. PRINT REGN-NO, AVG
Step 6. STOP.

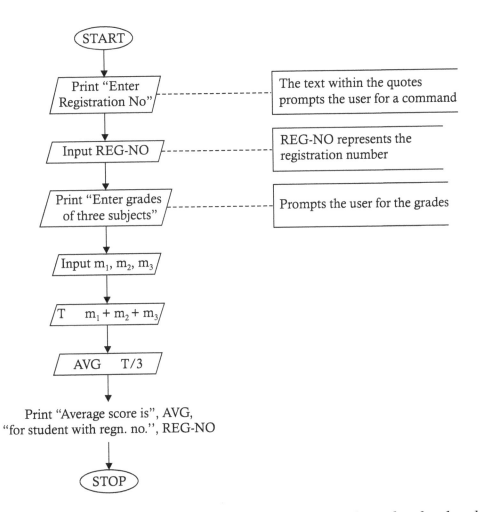

The text within the quotes prompts the user for a command

REG-NO represents the registration number

Prompts the user for the grades

Problem 1.9. *Draw a flowchart to accept the item's code, stock on hand, and the rate per unit of stock in a department store and display the stock value of the store.*

Task Analysis. The inputs required to determine the stock value of the store are the stock on hand and the rate per unit of stock, which are multiplied together to determine the stock value. The item's code is used as the identification data.

The algorithm corresponding to the solution for Problem 1.9 is as follows:

Step 1. INPUT TO I CODE
Step 2. INPUT TO SOH (SOH stands for "stock on hand")
Step 3. INPUT TO RATE

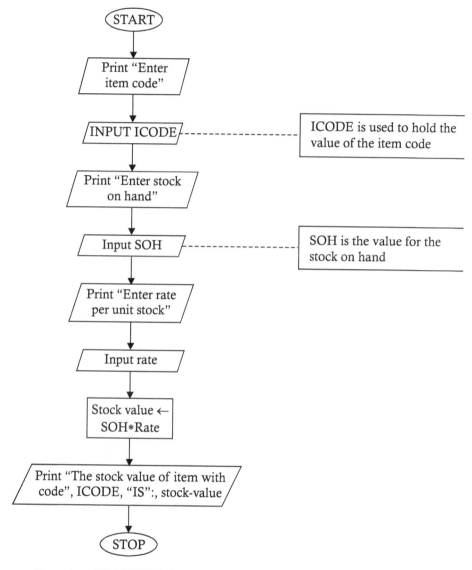

ICODE is used to hold the value of the item code

SOH is the value for the stock on hand

Step 4. COMPUTE STOCK-VALUE ← SOH*RATE
Step 5. PRINT STOCK-VALUE, ICODE
Step 6. STOP

Problem 1.10. *Draw a flowchart to determine the volume V_2 of a certain mass of gas at a pressure P_2 if the initial volume is V_1 at a pressure P_1, keeping the temperature constant.*

Task Analysis. From Boyle's law, we know that if the temperature remains constant, the volume of a given mass of gas varies inversely with its pressure. If V is a volume of a given mass of gas at a pressure P, then

$$V \propto \frac{1}{P} \text{, at a constant temperature}$$

i.e.,   PV = constant
Hence, we can write $P_1 V_1 = P_2 V_2$.

If the initial pressure and volume are known and the final pressure is also known for a given mass of gas, then the final volume V_2 can be determined from the formula.

$$V_2 = \frac{P_1 V_1}{P_2} \text{, the temperature being constant.}$$

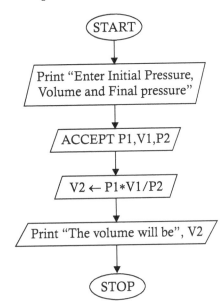

Hence, the inputs are P_1, V_1, and P_2, which gives us V_2 with the above formula.

The algorithm corresponding to Problem 1.10 is given below:

Step 1. INPUT TO P1, V1, P2
(P1 holds the value for the initial pressure, V1 holds the value of the initial volume, and P2 holds the value of the final pressure.)
Step 2. COMPUTE V2 ← P1*V1/P2
Step 3. PRINT V2
Step 4. STOP

Problem 1.11. *Draw a flowchart to show how to interchange the values of two variables.*

Task Analysis. The task of interchanging the values of two variables implies that the values contained by the variables are to be exchanged *i.e.*, the data value contained by the first variable should be contained by the second variable and that by the second variable should be contained by the first variable. If A and B are two variables, and if the values contained by them are 10 and 20 respectively, the problem is to make the contents of A and B, 20 and 10, respectively. This can be done simply with the help of a third variable used as an intermediate variable. The third variable holds the value of either A or B,

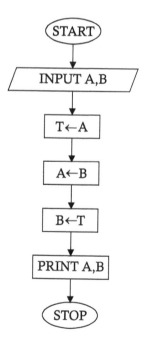

so that if the value of one variable is assigned to the other, the assignee's value is not lost forever but is available in the intermediate variable. Hence, it can then be assigned to the other variable.

The algorithm of the problem is as follows:

Step 1. ACCEPT A,B
Step 2. T ← A (Assign value in A to T)
Step 3. A ← B (Assign value in B to A)
Step 4. B ← T (Assign value in T to B)
Step 5. PRINT A,B
Step 6. STOP

EXERCISES

Construct flowcharts to show the steps involved to accomplish the following:

(i) Find the product of two numbers.

(ii) Find the remainder when one number is divided by the other.

(iii) Find the area of a parallelogram.

(iv) Find the area of the four walls of a rectangular room.

(v) Find the area and perimeter of a circular plot.

(vi) Find the area of a triangle based on the length of three sides.

(vii) Find the area and perimeter of a square.

(viii) Find the cost of fencing a rectangle at a given rate.

(ix) Find the surface area of a cone.

(x) Find the volume and surface area of a sphere.

(xi) Convert meters to kilometers.

(xii) Accept the rate for a dozen bananas and the quantity required to determine the cost.

(xiii) Find the cost of a flat having the floor space of the following pattern:

(xiv) Determine the acceleration due to gravity (g), where g can be obtained from the following formula:

$$T = 2\pi \sqrt{\frac{l}{g}}$$

where   T = Time period of a simple pendulum

and l = Effective length of the simple pendulum

(xv) Obtain the equivalent Fahrenheit temperature of a temperature given in Celsius where the relationship between the two scales of temperature is

$$\frac{C}{5} = \frac{F - 32}{9},$$

where   C = Temperature in Celsius

F = Temperature in Fahrenheit

2

PROBLEMS INVOLVING SELECTION

INTRODUCTION

This chapter deals with problems involving decision-making. This process of decision-making is implemented through a logic structure called *selection*. Here a *predicate*, also called a *condition*, is tested to see if it is true or false. If it is true, a course of action is specified for it; if it is found to be false, an alternative course of action is expressed. We can express this process using flowchart notation.

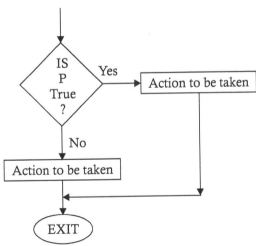

Note that a course of action may involve one or more sequences of operations, and there should be a common meeting point to satisfy the single rule pointed to by the connector containing the word "Exit." A flowchart may contain any number of decision boxes depending on the processing requirements, and the boxes may appear in any sequence depending on the program logic decided. For example, a number of decision boxes may follow one another. The following flowcharts provide an explanation of the logic to clarify this concept.

Problem 2.1. *Develop a flowchart to show how the profit or loss for a sale can be obtained.*

Task Analysis. The profit or loss for a sale can be obtained if the cost price and sale price are known. However, there is a need to make a decision here. If the cost price is more than the sale price, then it indicates a loss in the process; otherwise, there will be either zero profit (no profit or a loss) or some profit.

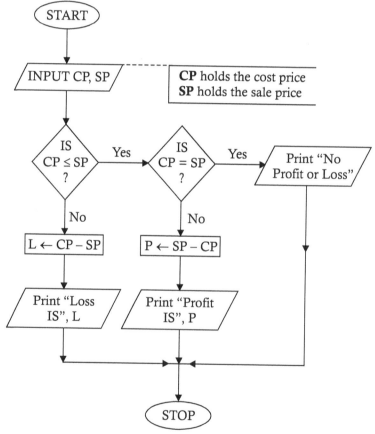

The algorithm corresponding to Problem 2.1 is given below:

Step 1.   INPUT TO CP, SP
Step 2.   IF CP <= SP

```
        THEN
                IF CP = SP
                        PRINT "NO PROFIT OR LOSS"
                ELSE
        COMPUTE P ← SP – CP
                PRINT "PROFIT IS"; P
        END-IF
    ELSE
            COMPUTE L ← CP – SP
            PRINT "LOSS IS"; L
    END-IF
```

Step 3. STOP

Problem 2.2. *Construct a procedure to show how to determine the greater of two given numbers.*

Task Analysis. We must determine the larger of two numbers. The task is to compare the given numbers to find the greater of them.

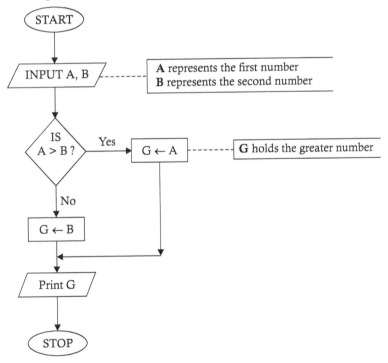

Note: Here we have assumed that the given numbers are different numbers.

The algorithm corresponding to Problem 2.2 is given below:

Step 1. INPUT TO A, B
Step 2. IF A > B
       THEN G ← A
   ELSE
      G ← B
   END-IF
Step 3. PRINT G
Step 4. STOP

Problem 2.3. *Construct a flowchart to determine whether a given number is even or odd.*

Task Analysis. We know that a number is an even number if it is completely divisible by 2. This means that if we perform integer division upon the given number, then the remainder of the division will be zero. To construct the flowchart, we accept a number as input, obtain the remainder of the integer division by taking it as the divisor, and then check whether the remainder is zero. If it is zero, then our conclusion will be that the number is an even number; otherwise, it will be an odd number.

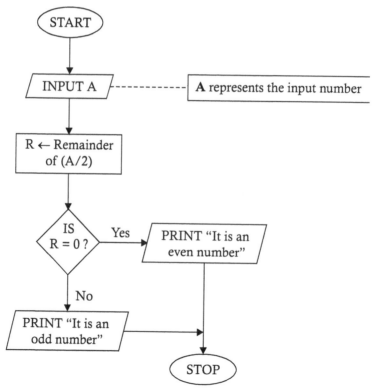

The algorithm corresponding to Problem 2.3 is shown below:

Step 1. INPUT TO A
Step 2. COMPUTE R ← Remainder of (A/2)
Step 3. IF R = 0
          THEN PRINT "It is an even number."
          ELSE
          PRINT "It is an odd number."
          END-IF
Step 4. STOP

Problem 2.4. *Determine the net payable amount on a sale. The net payable amount consists of the sale price plus sales tax. The sales tax is decided as*

a. *8% of the sale price for national items*

b. *18% of the sale price for foreign items*

Construct a flowchart to show how the net payable amount is determined.

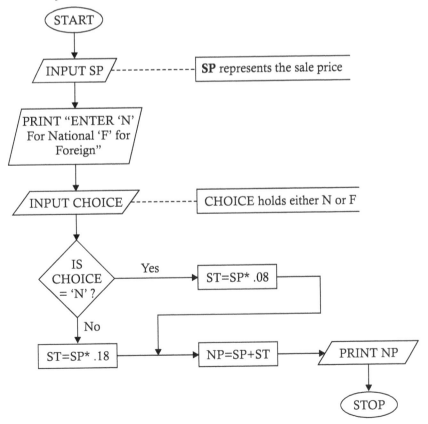

Task Analysis. We need to calculate the sales tax first by taking one of the two given rates. For this purpose, we require two inputs: the sale price of the item under consideration and the origin of the item. Let us assume that we provide "N" or "F" as the input to indicate "national" or "foreign," respectively.

The algorithm corresponding to Problem 2.4 is shown below:

Step 1. INPUT TO SP
Step 2. INPUT TO CHOICE ("N" for national and "F" for foreign)
Step 3. IF CHOICE = "N"
         THEN COMPUTE ST ← SP*.08
         ELSE
         COMPUTE ST ← SP*.18
         END-IF
         COMPUTE NP ← NP+ST
Step 4. PRINT NP
Step 5. STOP

Problem 2.5. *An equation with the form $ax^2 + bx + c = 0$ is known as a quadratic equation. Draw a flowchart to show how to solve a quadratic equation.*

Task Analysis. The values a, b, and c in the equation represent constant values. So $4x^2 - 17x - 15 = 0$ represents a quadratic equation where $a = 4$, $b = -17$, and $c = -15$. The values of x that satisfy a particular quadratic equation are known as the roots of the equation. The roots may be calculated by substituting the values of a, b, and c into the following two formulas:

$$x_1 = (-b + \sqrt{b^2 - 4ac})/2a$$
$$x_2 = (-b + \sqrt{b^2 - 4ac})/2a$$

The expression $b^2 - 4ac$ is called the *determinant* of the equation because it determines the nature of the roots of the equation. If the value of the determinant is less than zero, then the roots of the equation x_1 and x_2, are imaginary (complex) numbers. To solve a quadratic equation, we should allow the user to enter the values for a, b, and c. If the discriminant is less than zero, then a message should be displayed stating that the roots are imaginary; otherwise, the program should proceed to calculate and display the two roots of the equation.

The algorithm corresponding to Problem 2.5 is as follows:

Step 1. INPUT TO A, B, C
Step 2. COMPUTE D ← (B*B – 4*A*C) (Calculate the value of the discriminant) and store in D

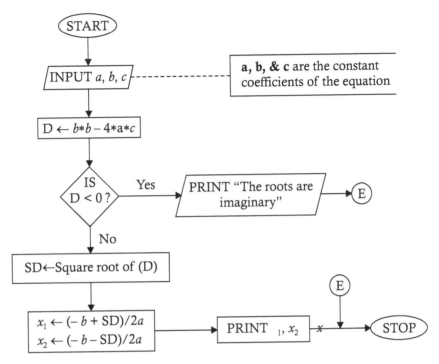

Step 3. IF D < 0
        THEN PRINT "THE ROOTS ARE IMAGINARY"
        ELSE
            COMPUTE SD ← SQUARE-ROOT (D)
        END-IF
Step 4. COMPUTE XI ← (– b + SD)/2∗A
Step 5. COMPUTE X2 ← (– b – SD)/2∗A
Step 6. PRINT XI, X2
Step 7. STOP

Problem 2.6. *Write a program to categorize the shape of a quadrilateral as either a square, rhombus, rectangle, parallelogram, or irregular quadrilateral, having input the lengths of the four sides and one internal angle.*

Task Analysis. To make the decision about the shape of a quadrilateral, we need to know the definitions of the quadrilaterals. A quadrilateral is called a square if all the sides are of equal length and each of the internal angles is a right angle. A quadrilateral is called a rhombus if the lengths of all sides are the same and no angle is a right angle. If only one internal angle is given and the sides are given, then in the case where all sides are of the same length and the internal angle is not a right angle, then the quadrilateral must be a rhombus. If the internal angle is a right angle and the sides are of same length, then it must be a square. If the opposite sides are of the same length and the internal angle is a right angle, then it must be a rectangle; if the opposite sides are of same length and the internal angle is not a right angle, then it must be a parallelogram. If none of the above conditions are satisfied, then the quadrilateral is an irregular quadrilateral. The steps of the logic are shown in the flowchart.

The algorithm corresponding to Problem 2.6 is given below.

AB, BC, CD, and DA are the lengths of the sides of a quadrilateral and I is the measure of an internal angle. This algorithm decides the shape of the quadrilateral.

Step 1. ACCEPT AB, BC, CD, DA, I
Step 2. IF AB = BC
      THEN IF AB = CD
         THEN IF BC = DA
            THEN IF I = 90
               THEN PRINT "IT'S A SQUARE"
             ELSE
               PRINT "IT'S A RHOMBUS"
             END-IF
             ELSE
               PRINT "IT'S AN IRREGULAR QUADRILATERAL"
             END-IF
             ELSE
               PRINT "IT'S AN IRREGULAR QUADRILATERAL"
             END-IF
      ELSE
         IF AB = CD
           THEN IF BC = DA
              THEN IF I = 90
                 THEN PRINT "IT'S A RECTANGLE"
               ELSE
                 PRINT "IT'S A PARALLELOGRAM"
               END-IF
              ELSE
                PRINT "IT'S AN IRREGULAR QUADRILATERAL"
              END-IF
           ELSE
              PRINT "IT'S AN IRREGULAR QUADRILATERAL"
      END-IF
Step 3. STOP

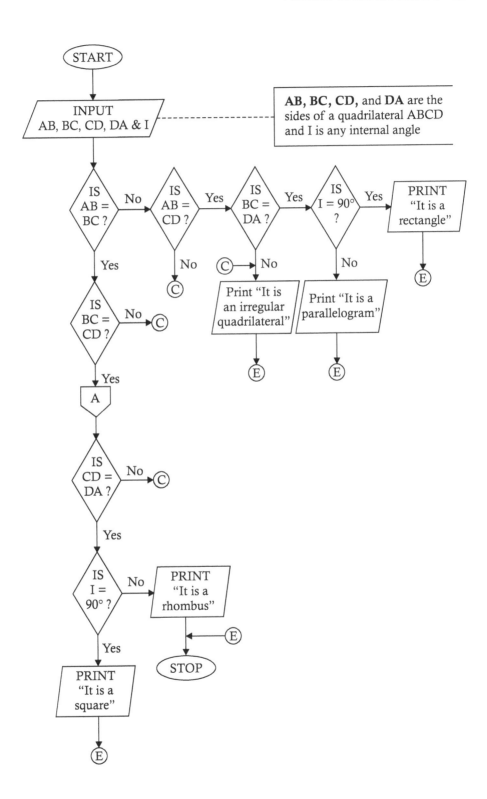

Problem 2.7. *The grades in a certain class are determined by coursework and a written examination. Both components of the assessment carry a maximum of 50 points.*

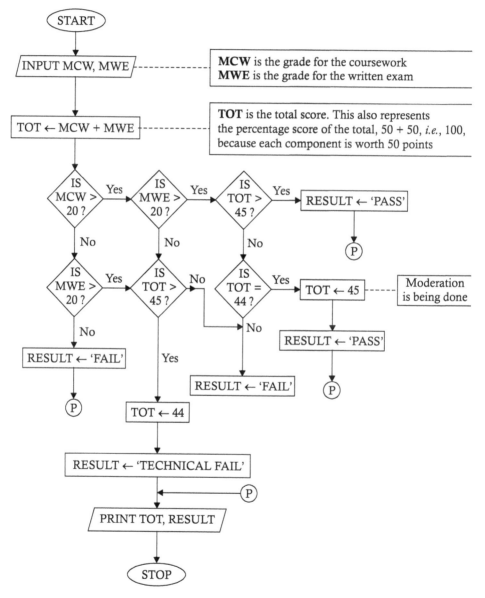

The following rules are applied by the examiners to determine whether a student passes:

(i) *A student must score a total of 45% or more in order to pass*

(ii) *A total grade of 44% is moderated to 45%*

(iii) *Each component must be passed with a minimum of 20 points*

(iv) *If a student scores 45% or more, but does not achieve the minimum grade in one component, he is given a technical fail of 44%, which is not moderated to 45%.*

Develop a flowchart showing how to input the grades for each component and output the final grade and the result.

Task Analysis. The readily available facts about a student are the grades obtained for the coursework and written examination. These can be supplied as the input to obtain the desired output. The procedure includes finding the total score and then checking to determine whether it is "pass," "fail," or "technical fail." A *moderation, i.e.*, an increment, of the final score is also done, if required, when a student obtains a total score of 44%. Our objective is to show the solution interactively for one student at a time. No input is needed to identify the student.

The algorithm corresponding to Problem 2.7 is given below:

Step 1. INPUT TO MCW, MWE (Accept the grades of the coursework and that of the written examination)

Step 2. TOT ← MCW + MWE (Store the sum of MCW and MWE in TOT)

Step 3. IF MCW > 20
      THEN IF MWE > 20
            THEN IF TOT > 45
                  THEN RESULT ← "Pass"
                        (Store "PASS" in RESULT)
                  ELSE
                     IF TOT = 44
                        THEN RESULT ← 45
                           (Moderation of 44 to make it 45)
                              RESULT ← "PASS"
                  ELSE
                     RESULT ← "FAIL"
                  END-IF
                    END-IF
            ELSE
               IF TOT > 45
                  THEN
                     TOT ← 44

RESULT ← "TECHNICAL FAIL"
                    END-IF
                    END-IF
               ELSE
                  IF MWE > 20
                     THEN
                     TOT ← 44
                        RESULT ← "TECHNICAL FAIL"
                  END-IF
          END-IF
Step 4. PRINT TOT, RESULT
Step 5. STOP

Problem 2.8. *The following rules are used to calculate the bonus for the employees of an organization.*

(i) *If the pay is more than $3,000, the bonus amount is fixed, and it is equal to $300.*

(ii) *If the pay is more than $1,600, but less than or equal to $3,000, the bonus will be 10% of the pay subject to a maximum of $240.*

(iii) *If the pay is less than or equal to $1,600, the bonus is 15% of pay, subject to a minimum of $100.*

Task Analysis. The input required here is the pay amount that an employee gets. On the basis of the pay, we can determine the bonus amount. The "subject to maximum" or the "subject to minimum" clause implies that the calculated amount should be compared with the maximum or minimum limit. If it is more than the maximum limit or less than the minimum limit, then the maximum limit or the minimum limit will be treated as the legitimate value.

The algorithm corresponding to Problem 2.8 is given below:

Step 1. INPUT TO PAY
Step 2. IF PAY > 3000
            THEN BONUS ← 300
         ELSE
            IF PAY > 1600
               THEN BONUS ← PAY* 10/100
                  IF BONUS > 240
                     THEN
                        BONUS ← 240
                  END-IF
            ELSE

$$BONUS \leftarrow PAY * 15/100$$
$$IF\ BONUS < 100$$
$$BONUS \leftarrow 100$$
END-IF
END-IF
END-IF

Step 3. PRINT BONUS
Step 4. STOP

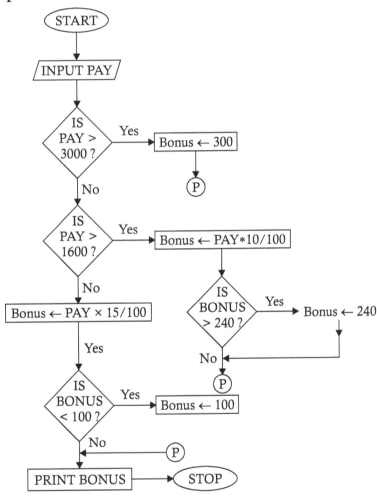

Problem 2.9. *A certain steel is graded according to the following conditions:*

(i) *Rockwell hardness > 50*
(ii) *Carbon content > 0.7*
(iii) *Tensile strength > 5600 kg/cm^2*

The steel is graded as follows:

a. *Grade 10, if all the conditions are satisfied*
b. *Grade 9, if conditions (i) and (ii) are satisfied*
c. *Grade 8, if conditions (ii) and (iii) are satisfied*
d. *Grade 7, if conditions (i) and (iii) are satisfied*
e. *Grade 0, otherwise*

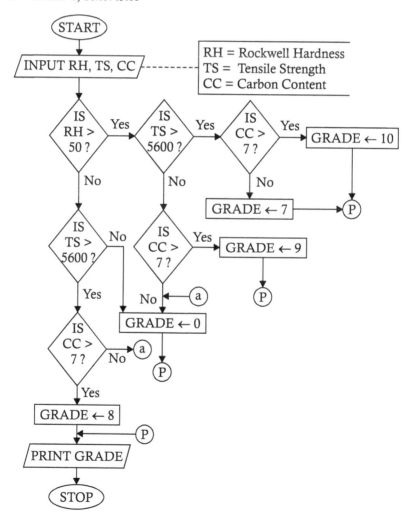

Task Analysis. We must determine the grade of the steel on the basis of the values of three characteristics, namely, the Rockwell hardness, carbon content, and tensile strength. The values of these three features are the input.

The algorithm corresponding to Problem 2.9 is given below:

Step 1. INPUT TO RH, TS, CC
Step 2. IF RH > 50
        THEN IF TS > 5600
                THEN IF CC > 0.7
                        THEN GRADE ← 10
                        ELSE
                            GRADE ← 7
                        END-IF
            ELSE
              IF CC > 0.7
                THEN GRADE ← 9
              ELSE
                GRADE ← 0
              END-IF
            END-IF
        ELSE
            IF TS > 5600
              THEN IF CC > 0.7
                    THEN GRADE ← 8
                    ELSE
                      GRADE ← 0
                  END-IF
              ELSE
                GRADE ← 0
            END-IF
Step 3. PRINT GRADE
Step 4. STOP

Problem 2.10. *Construct a flowchart to show how the greatest of the three given numbers can be obtained.*

Task Analysis. This problem is similar to the problem for finding the greater of two given numbers. The only difference is that two successive comparisons are needed because three numbers cannot be compared at a time.

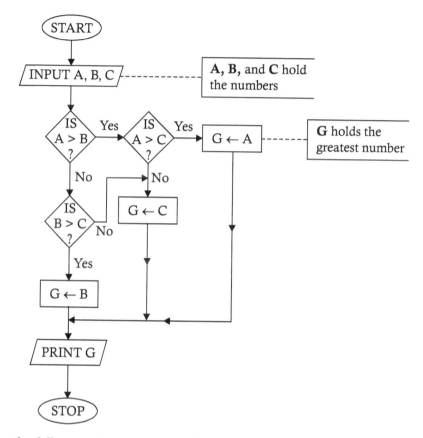

The following algorithm shows the procedure to follow for Problem 2.10:

Step 1. INPUT TO A, B, C
        (Accept three numbers for A, B, and C)
Step 2. IF A > B
        THEN IF A > C
                THEN G ← A
                  (G holds the desired number)
                ELSE
                    G ← C
                END-IF
        ELSE
            IF B > C
                THEN G ← B
            ELSE
                G ← C
            END-IF

END-IF

Step 3. PRINT "THE GREATEST OF THE GIVEN NUMBERS IS", G

Step 4. STOP

Problem 2.11. *A bookseller offers two rates of commissions. If the price of a book is below $100, the rate of commission is 12% of the price, otherwise, it is 18% of the price. Develop a procedure to determine the discount and the net price of a book.*

Task Analysis. The outputs required are the discount and net price of a book. The only input required for this purpose is price of the book. The rates of the discount are constants (fixed). These rates can be used to develop formulas to calculate the discounts in the two different cases. The calculated discount can then be subtracted from the price of the book to obtain the net price.

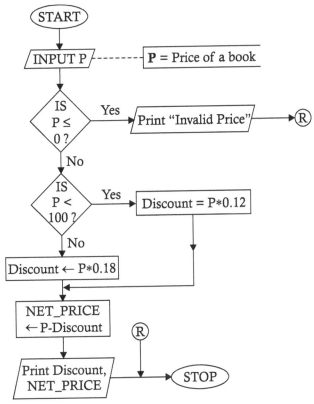

Note that the procedure suggests the printing of a message when some absurd input is provided.

The algorithm corresponding to Problem 2.11 is given below:

Step 1. INPUT TO P
             (Accept the price of a book in P)
Step 2. IF P <= 0
                 THEN PRINT "INVALID PRICE"
             ELSE
                 IF P < 100
             COMPUTE D ← P*0.12 (Store the calculated discount in D)
                 ELSE
             COMPUTE D ← P*0.18
                 END-IF
             END-IF
Step 3. COMPUTE NET_PRICE ← P – D
Step 4. PRINT D, NET_PRICE
Step 5. STOP

EXERCISES

Construct flowcharts for the following problems:

(i) Print a currency conversion table for pounds, francs, marks, and lire to dollars.

(ii) Find whether a given year is a leap year.

   Hint. A year is said to be a leap year if it is either divisible by 4 but not by 100 or divisible by 400.

(iii) Validate a given year.

   Hints. The year in the date must be greater than zero, the months must lie between 1 and 12, and the days must lie between 1 and 31, depending on the month numbers.

(iv) Show the time required by an advertising agency for its advertising program to run in Boston and on National Public Radio and to display the amount to be paid by the agency for its advertisement.

(v) Calculate the commission of a salesman when sales and the region of the sales are given as input. The commission is calculated with the rules as follows:

(a) No commission, if sales < $9,000 in Region A

(b) 5.5% of sales < $7,000 in Region B and when sales < $13,000 in Region A

(c) 7.5% of sales when sales > = $14,000 in Region A and when sales > = $13,000 in Region B.

(vi) Accept three integers representing the angles of a triangle in degrees to determine whether they form a valid set of angles of a triangle. If it is not a valid set, then generate a message and terminate the process. If it is a valid set, then the process determines whether it is equiangular (all three angles are the same). It also determines if the triangle is right angled (has one angle with 90 degrees), obtuse angled (one angle above 90), or acute angled (all three angles are below 90 degrees). Finally, it shows conclusion about the triangle.

(vii) Accept the lengths of the three sides of a triangle to validate whether they can be the sides of a triangle and then classify the triangle as equilateral (all three sides are equal), scalene (all three sides are different), or isosceles (exactly two sides are equal), and then to see whether it is a right angled triangle (the sum of the squares of two sides is equal to the square of the third side.)

Hint. Three numbers are valid as the sides of a triangle if each one is positive and the sum of every two numbers is greater than the third.

(viii) Allow the user to perform a simple task on a calculator on the basis of a given choice as follows:

+, −, ×, /, or % representing the arithmetic operators

A   Average of two numbers

X   Maximum of two numbers

M   Minimum of two numbers

S   Square of two numbers

Q   Quit

(ix) An electricity board charges the following rates to domestic users to discourage large consumption of energy:

for the first 100 units—$.85 per unit

for the next 200 units—$1.45 per unit

Beyond 300 units—$1.85 per unit

All users are charged a minimum of $ 500.00. If the total cost is more than $ 2,500.00, then an additional surcharge of 3% of the total cost is added to the total cost to determine the final bill.

(x) To determine and print the minimum number of currency notes of the denominations: $1, $5, $10, $20, $50, $100, $500 and $1000 required to pay any given amount.

CHAPTER 3

PROBLEMS INVOLVING LOOPING

INTRODUCTION

In the flowcharts of the preceding chapter, we demonstrated the sequence and selection logic structures. We now move to the iteration logic structure.

The term *iteration* means repetition. Sometimes, a procedure should be executed repeatedly. All procedures should be built so that they can be repeated as many times as needed. We should not develop procedures to execute only once. Otherwise, calculators could be sufficient to obtain the results. An iterative logic structure is also known as a *loop*. *Looping* means repeating a set of operations to obtain a result repeatedly.

An iteration may be implemented in two ways: a pre-test iteration and post-test iteration. In case of a *pre-test iteration*, a predicate is tested to decide whether a set of operations is to be performed or not. If the condition implied by the predicate is true, then the desired operations are performed. If it is false, then the iteration is terminated. This is shown in the following diagram.

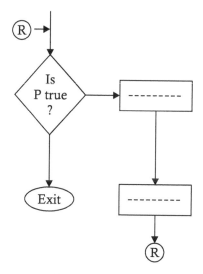

For a post-test iteration, the predicate is tested after performing a set of operations once to decide whether to repeat the set of operations or to terminate the repetition. If the condition happens to be true, then the set of operations is repeated; otherwise, it is not repeated. The diagrammatic structure of this logic is as follows.

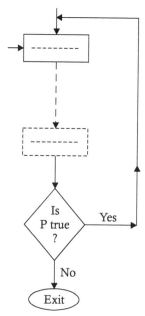

Note that the operations in the loop must be performed at least once in the case of a post-test iteration.

The concept of looping is demonstrated in the following flowchart. Of course, there should be a condition for normal termination. Let us assume that the repetitive task of calculating the discounts and net prices is terminated when we provide negative or zero as the price for the input. Such absurd values are justified for the termination of loops so that the procedure can remain valid for any possible value of the price. We usually use out-connectors and in-connectors with the same label to demonstrate the end point and start point of a loop. These are shown in the flowchart of Problem 2.11.

The algorithm corresponding to the flowchart is below:

Step 1. REPEAT STEPS 2 THROUGH 6 (Start Loop)
Step 2. INPUT TO P
Step 3. IF P ≤ 0 THEN EXIT (Stop Repetition, *i.e.*, transfer the control to STOP).

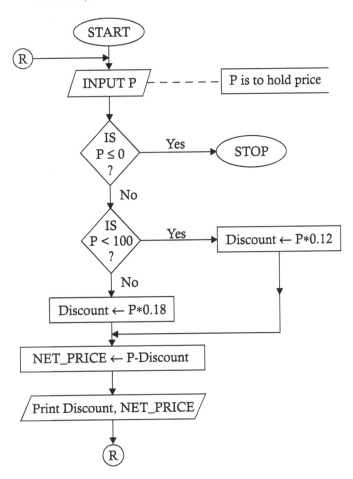

Step 4. If P < 100
  THEN COMPUTE D ← P*0.12
  ELSE COMPUTE D ← P*0.18
  END-IF
Step 5. COMPUTE NET_PRICE ← P – D
Step 6. PRINT D, NET_PRICE (End of loop)
Step 7. STOP

Note that the out-connector Ⓡ shows the end point of the loop and the in-connector. Ⓡ⟶ shows the start point of the loop. The operations starting from the point of the accepting the input price up to the points of printing the output discount and net price are within the loop. It could have been demonstrated without using connectors.

However, we prefer the first flowchart to the following one, because if the flowchart cannot be accommodated on a single page (or in a continuous structure on a single page), it would be difficult or impossible difficult to connect the start point and the end point.

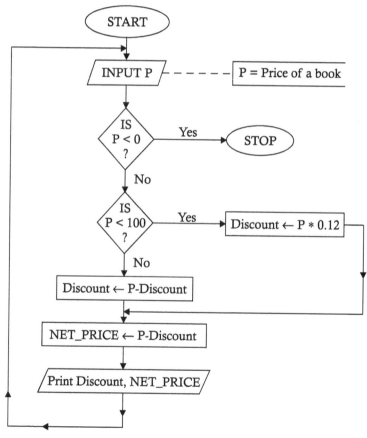

Problem 3.1. *The salesmen of a sales firm are given a commission on sales achieved, using the following rules:*

Sales	Rate of commission
<= 5,000	7% of sales
> 5,000 but <= 10,000	9% of sales + $500
> 10,000 but <= 20,000	11% of sales + $1,000
> 20,000 but <= 25,000	13% of sales + $2,000
> 25,000	15% of sales + $4,000

Devise a procedure to calculate the commission of the salesmen.

Task Analysis. The output required is the commission earned by a salesman. The only input required is the amount of the sale. A number of decision-making steps are involved, and the process is likely to be repeated a number of times. Let us assume that the process can be terminated when the amount of the sale is zero or negative. The procedure is illustrated in the following flowchart.

The algorithm corresponding to Problem 3.1 is given below:

Step 1.   REPEAT STEPS 2 THROUGH 5
Step 2.   INPUT TO S
          (Accept sales amount in S)
Step 3.   If S <= 0
        THEN EXIT
        END-IF
Step 4.   IF S <= 5000
        THEN COMPUTE COM ← S * .07
        ELSE
          IF S <= 10000
            THEN COMPUTE COM ← S * .09 + 500
          ELSE
            IF S <= 20000
              THEN COMPUTE COM ← S * 0.11 + 1000
            ELSE
              IF S <= 25000
                THEN COMPUTE COM ← S * 0.13 + 2000
              ELSE
                COMPUTE COM ← S * 0.15 + 4000
              END-IF
            END-IF
          END-IF
        END-IF
Step 5.   PRINT COM
Step 6.   STOP

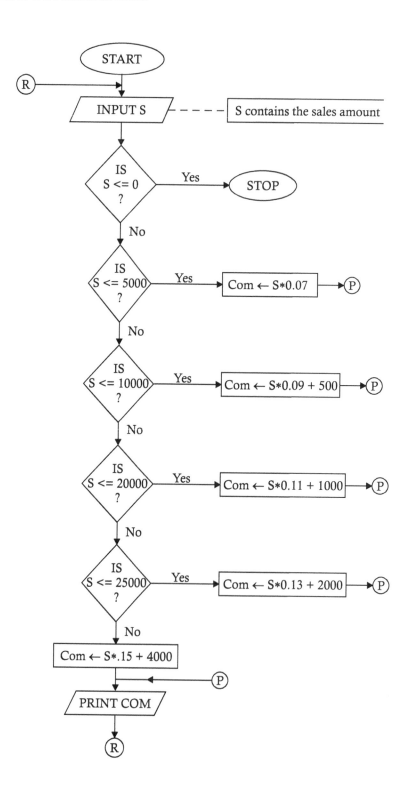

Problem 3.2. *A sales organization offers a fixed salary and a percentage of sales as a commission to determine the monthly remuneration of an employee under the following conditions.*

If the sales amount of an employee exceeds $5,000, then the commission is 12% of the sales that exceed $5,000; otherwise, it is nil. Draw a flowchart to show how the remuneration of an employee is decided.

Task Analysis. The remuneration of an employee consists of two parts: a fixed salary part and a commission part that depends on the sales amount. We use the fixed salary part and the sales amount as input to determine the commission and hence, the remuneration.

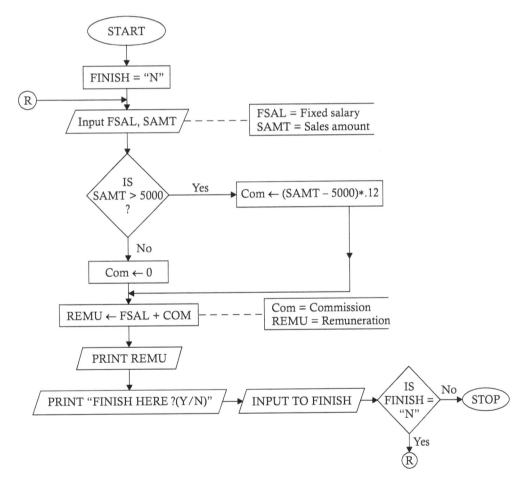

The algorithm corresponding to Problem 3.2 is given below:

Step 1. FINISH ← "N"
Step 2. REPEAT STEPS 3 THROUGH 9 WHILE FINISH = "N"
Step 3. INPUT TO FSAL, SAMT
Step 4. IF SAMT > 5000
      THEN COMPUTE COM ← (SAMT − 5000) * .12
    ELSE
      COM ← 0
    END-IF
Step 5. COMPUTE REMU ← FSAL + COM
Step 6. PRINT "REMUNERATION IS", REMU
Step 7. PRINT "FINISH (Y/N)?"
Step 8. INPUT TO FINISH
Step 9. IF FINISH = "Y"
    THEN EXIT
    END-IF
Step 10. STOP

Problem 3.3. *A labor contractor pays the workers at the end of each week according to the rules given below:*

For the first 35 hours of work, the rate of pay is $15 per hour; for the next 25 hours, the rate of pay is $18 per hour; for the rest, the rate of pay is $26 per hour. No worker is allowed to work for more than 80 hours in a week. Develop a flowchart to show how the wages of the workers can be calculated on the basis of valid inputs.

Task Analysis. The input required is the total number of hours worked. The rates of payment depend on the different numbers of hours worked. The total hours worked may be considered valid if the number lies in the range of 0 through 80. Our procedure for evaluating the wage consists of the (*i*) validation of the hours worked, (*ii*) identifying the category to which the hours worked pertain, and then (*iii*) applying different rates to calculate the wage. The procedure is shown within a loop, and it is terminated when zero or a negative value is given as the input against hours worked.

The algorithm corresponding to Problem 3.3 is given below:

Step 1. REPEAT STEPS 2 THROUGH 6
Step 2. INPUT TO TH
Step 3. IF TH <= 0
    THEN EXIT
    END-IF

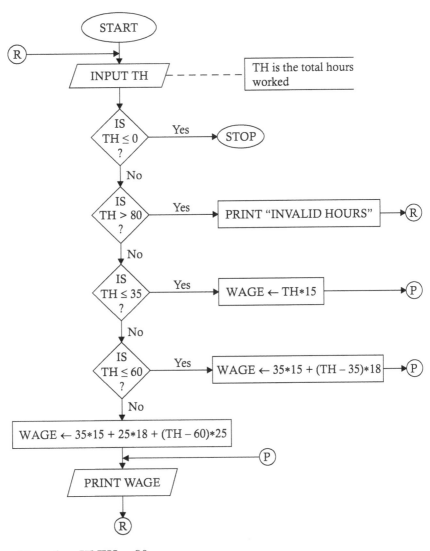

Step 4. IF TH > 80
      THEN PRINT "INVALID HOURS"
      CONTINUE
    END-IF
Step 5. IF TH <= 35
      THEN COMPUTE WAGE ← TH*15
    ELSE
      IF TH <= 60
         THEN COMPUTE WAGE ← 35*15 + (TH–35)*18

         ELSE

             COMPUTE WAGE ← 35*15 + 25*18 + (TH–60)*25

         END-IF

         END-IF

Step 6. PRINT "WAGE IS", WAGE

Step 7. STOP

Problem 3.4. *In New Delhi, the telephone bill is calculated according to the following rules for the first 300 calls, the bill is fixed and it is equal to Rs. 500; for the next 65 calls, the rate per call is Re. 0.95; for the next 90 calls, the rate per call is Rs. 1.50; for calls beyond that the rate per call is Rs. 2.25 per call.*

Develop a flowchart to show how the telephone bill is calculated.

Task Analysis. The input required is the number of calls and the output required is the total bill for the telephone calls. Note that the rates vary only for the excess number of calls in a particular category. The following flowchart demonstrates the formulas for calculating the bill.

    The algorithm of the solution for Problem 3.4 is given below:

Step 1. REPEAT STEPS 2 THROUGH 5 UNTIL CALLS < 0

Step 2. INPUT TO CALLS

Step 3. IF CALLS < 0 THEN EXIT

Step 4. IF CALLS < = 300

        THEN BILL ← 500

      ELSE

        IF CALLS <= 365

          THEN COMPUTE BILL ← 500 + (CALLS – 300) * 0.95

        ELSE

          IF CALLS <= 455

          THEN COMPUTE BILL ← 500 + 65*0.95 + (CALLS – 365)*1.50

        ELSE

          COMPUTE BILL ← 500 + 65*0.95 + 90*1.50 + (CALLS – 455)*2.25

          END-IF

        END-IF

      END-IF

Step 5. PRINT "THE TELEPHONE BILL IS", BILL

Step 6. STOP

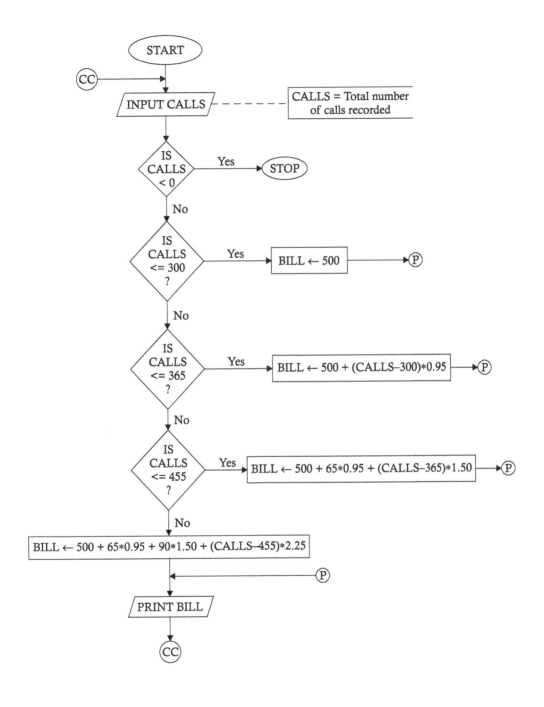

Problem 3.5. *The cost of living (CL), the travel allowance (TA), and medical allowance (MA) of the employees of a company are decided according to the following rules:*

CL = 123.75% of the Basic Pay, subject to a minimum of $2,000 and a maximum of $5,000.
TA = 57.5% of the Basic Pay, subject to a minimum of $300.
MA = 73.5% of the Basic Pay, subject to a maximum of $2,000.
Draw a flowchart to show how CL, TA, and MA are calculated.

Task Analysis. The allowances are based on the Basic Pay of an employee. Our input will be the basic pay of the employee for whom the allowances are to be determined. The statement "123.75% of the basic pay subject to a minimum of $2,000 and a maximum of $5,000" implies that 123.75% of the basic bay is calculated first and then the calculated value is compared with 2,000; if it is less than $2,000, then the company promises to pay $2,000; if it is not less than $2,000 then it will be compared with $5,000; if it exceeds $5,000, the company will not pay the excess amount, *i.e.*, it agrees to pay, at most, $5,000: If the calculated value lies in between the two given limits, then that amount will be given as CL. Similarly, the other allowances will be determined. This is demonstrated in the flowchart given on next page.

The algorithm corresponding to the above problem has been given below:

Step 1. CH ← "Y"
Step 2. REPEAT STEPS 3 THROUGH 14 WHILE CH = "Y"
Step 3. INPUT TO BASIC
Step 4. COMPUTE CL ← BASIC*123.75/100
Step 5. IF CL < 2000
    THEN CL ← 2000
  ELSE
   IF CL > 5000
    THEN CL ← 5000
   END-IF
  END-IF
Step 6. PRINT CL
Step 7. COMPUTE TA ← BASIC*57.5/100
Step 8. IF TA < 300
    THEN TA ← 300
  END-IF

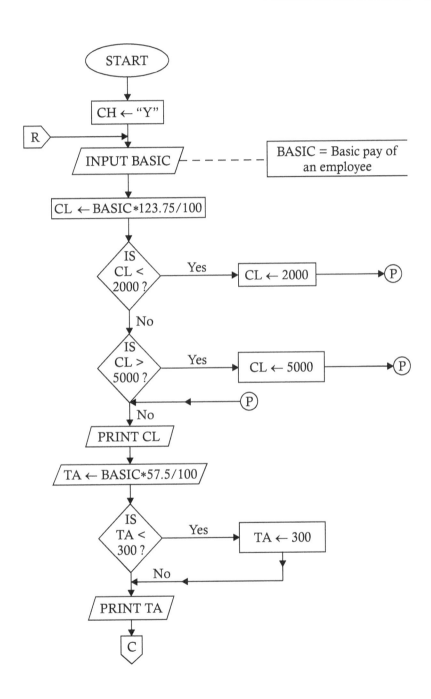

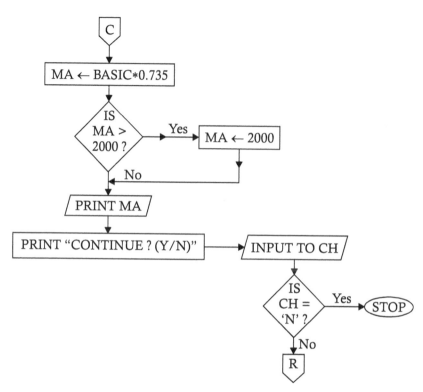

Step 9. COMPUTE MA ← BASIC*0.735
Step 10. IF MA > 2000
        THEN MA ← 2000
        END-IF
Step 11. PRINT MA
Step 12. PRINT "CONTINUE? (Y/N)"
Step 13. INPUT TO CH
Step 14. IF CH = "N"
        THEN EXIT
        END-IF
Step 15. STOP

Problem 3.6. *Devise a procedure to find the sum of first n natural numbers, where n is any given integer, without using a formula.*

Task Analysis. Natural numbers are those numbers that are obtained through sequential counting. The starting number here for the summation process is 1, the next number is 2 and so on, until we reach n—the number of natural numbers to be summed. The numbers to be added are known as inputs and can be generated by instructing the computer. We assign the value 1 to a variable to simulate the first natural number. We then add the value of the variable to an accumulator. The accumulator must then contain some initial value to make the summation process semantically correct, *i.e.*, meaningful. This initial value must be 0 in this case because we are adding the first number. We can then increase the value of the variable containing the first natural number by 1. This next number, which is 2 in this case, can then be added to the current value of the accumulator to obtain the sum of first two natural numbers. In this way, we can continue the generation and summation process until we add up all the natural numbers, including N, for some given value of N. But we must also keep a count of the numbers that are being added; otherwise we will not be able to decide whether we have added the desired N numbers or not. A variable is used here as a counter. This counter must be initialized to zero first, from which we can increment its value each time by 1 when we add some number to the value of the accumulator.

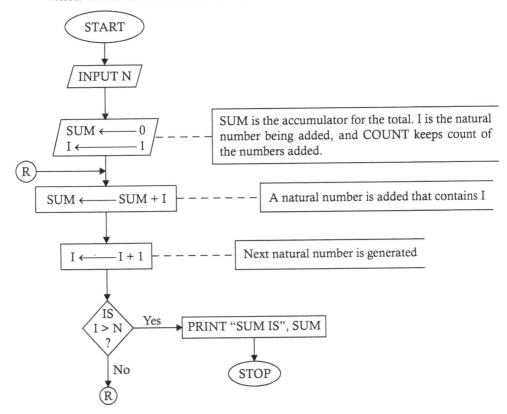

The algorithm corresponding to Problem 3.6 is shown below:

Step 1. INPUT "ENTER NUMBER OF TERMS TO ADD" TO N
Step 2. SUM ← 0 [INITIALIZATION]
Step 3. I ← 1 [INITIALIZATION]
Step 4. REPEAT STEPS 5 THROUGH 6 WHILE I <= N.
Step 5. COMPUTE SUM ← SUM + I
Step 6. COMPUTE I ← I + 1
Step 7. PRINT "THE SUM IS", SUM
Step 8. STOP

Problem 3.7. *Draw a flowchart to show how to obtain the sum of the first 30 natural numbers.*

Task Analysis. This problem is similar to Problem 3.6. The only difference is that the number of natural numbers to be added up is given as a constant (30). We do not need input from the user.

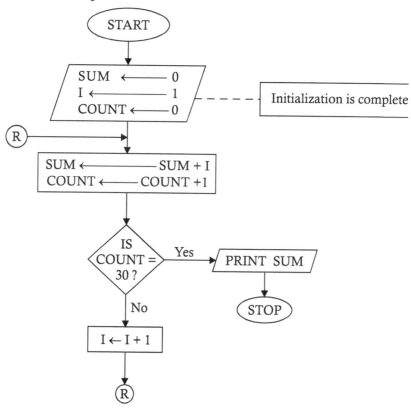

The algorithm corresponding to Problem 3.7 is shown below:

Step 1. SUM ← 0, I ← 1, COUNT ← 0
[Initialize the variables required]
Step 2. REPEAT STEPS 3 THROUGH 5 WHILE COUNT <= 30
Step 3. COMPUTE SUM ← SUM + I
Step 4. COMPUTE COUNT ← COUNT + 1
Step 5. COMPUTE I ← I + 1
Step 6. PRINT "THE SUM IS", SUM
Step 7. STOP

Problem 3.8. *Draw a flowchart to show how to find the product of first 10 natural numbers.*

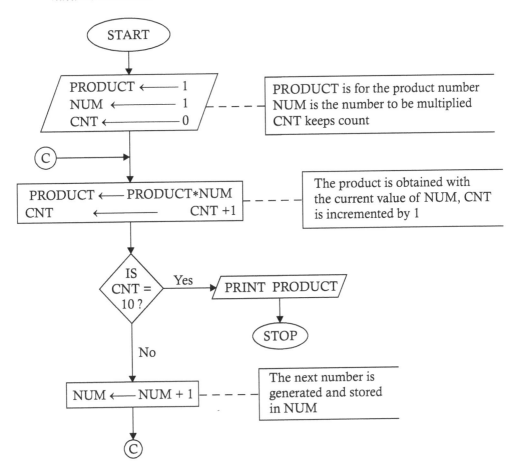

Task Analysis. We require the product of the first 10 natural numbers. The natural numbers are defined in the task analysis of Problem 3.6, so the natural numbers can be generated similarly. To hold the product, we require a location that is initialized with 1 so that we can specify how to obtain the new product by multiplying the current product by the natural number currently in use. This is because only the initial value 1 will keep the content of the location for the product unchanged when the value of the product location is multiplied by 1.

The algorithm showing solution to Problem 3.8 is as follows:

Step 1. PRODUCT ← 1, NUM ← 1, CNT ← 0
(Initialize the variables required)
Step 2. REPEAT STEPS 3 THROUGH 5 WHILE CNT <= 10
Step 3. COMPUTE PRODUCT ← PRODUCT*NUM
Step 4. COMPUTE CNT ← CNT + 1
(Increment the Counter)
Step 5. COMPUTE NUM ← NUM + 1 (The next number is generated)
Step 6. PRINT "THE PRODUCT IS", PRODUCT
Step 7. STOP

Problem 3.9. *Draw a flowchart to find the sum of first 15 even natural numbers.*

Task Analysis. We know that the first natural even number is 2 and the next natural even number, *i.e.*, the second even number, can be obtained by adding 2 to the first natural number. The successive natural even numbers can be obtained by adding 2 to the preceding natural even number. These even numbers can be accumulated in a location by adding the generated even number each time to the accumulator, which contains zero.

A count of the numbers added will enable us to check whether first 15 even natural numbers have been added up or not. No input is required from the user during the time of execution.

The algorithm showing the solution of Problem 3.9. is given below:

Step 1. [Initialize the accumulator, counter and variable]
SUMM ← 0, CNT ← 0, NUM ← 2
Step 2. REPEAT STEPS 3 THROUGH 5 WHILE CNT < 15
Step 3. COMPUTE SUMM ← SUMM + NUM
Step 4. COMPUTE CNT ← CNT + 1
Step 5. COMPUTE NUM ← NUM + 2
Step 6. PRINT "THE DESIRED SUM IS", SUMM
Step 7. STOP

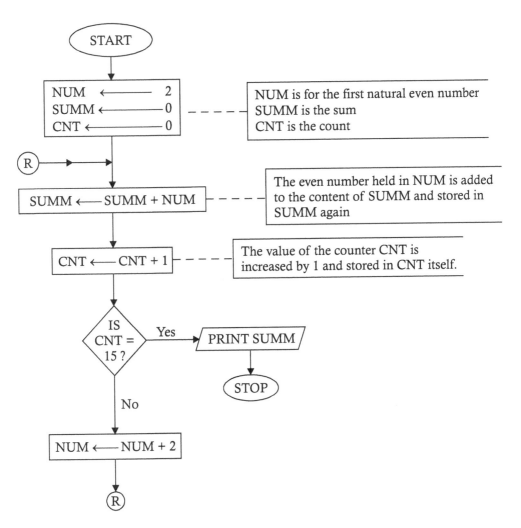

Problem 3.10. *Construct a flowchart to show how consecutive even numbers starting from 2 are summed up until the sum just exceeds 1000 and then show the sum and the number of even numbers added.*

Task Analysis. The starting input is given as the first even number and we are required to sum up the consecutive even numbers. These even numbers can be generated by adding 2 each time to the preceding even number, as shown earlier. The terminating condition is not a count, but the total of the even numbers being summed up when the total exceeds 1000. A count of the numbers added to make the sum exceeding 1000 is also required in the output, so we need to maintain a counter also. As the input data values can be generated through a procedure easily, we need not accept any input from the terminal during the time of execution.

The solution of Problem 3.10 is as follows:

Step 1. [Initialize the required variables]
SUMM ← 0, N ← 2, CNT ← 0
Step 2. REPEAT STEPS 2 THROUGH 5 UNTIL SUMM > 1000
Step 3. COMPUTE SUMM ← SUMM + N
Step 4. COMPUTE CNT ← CNT + 1
Step 5. COMPUTE N ← N + 2
Step 6. STOP

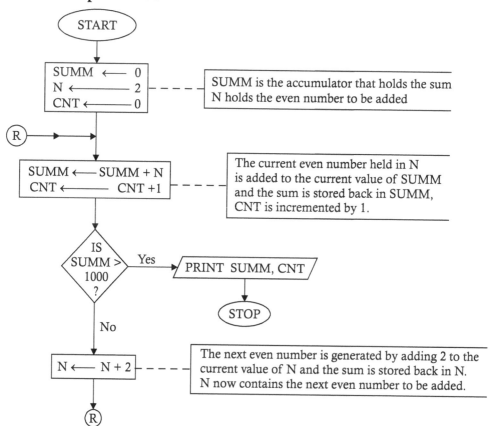

Problem 3.11. *Construct a flowchart to print the numbers below 100 that are divisible by 7.*

Task Analysis. The numbers below 100 divisible by 7 can be obtained in two ways. First, they can be obtained using the multiples of 7 below 100, and second, by taking the natural numbers from 1 to 100 and then by checking whether the number is divisible by 7. A number will be called divisible by 7 if the integer division of the number by 7 gives no remainder. The flowchart illustrated below is based on the second approach, where the natural numbers are generated and then tested for the divisibility.

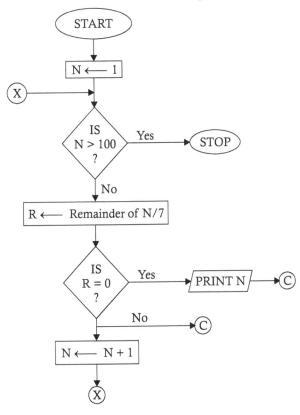

The solution of Problem 3.11 is shown in the following algorithm:

Step 1. [Initialize the variable that will contain the number]
N ← 1

Step 2. REPEAT STEPS 3 THROUGH 5 WHILE N <= 100

Step 3. COMPUTE R ← Remainder of (N/7)

Step 4. IF R = 0
THEN PRINT N
END-IF

Step 5. COMPUTE N ← N + 1
(Increment the value of N)

Step 6. STOP

Problem 3.12. *A used bicycle shop lends bicycles with the following rules:*

A deposit of $150 must be made before taking any bicycle from the shop. The charges for hiring depend on the month in which it is hired. If the number of days of hire exceeds 15, a discount of 11% is offered. The hire-rate is determined as per the following rules:

Month name	Rate/day (in $)
Jan. to Mar.	1.75
April to June	1.65
July to Sept.	1.50
Oct. to Dec.	1.15

In case of multiple day hiring, the rate is same for all days as on the first day of hiring. Develop a flowchart showing the logic to calculate the amount to be paid before taking any bicycle from the shop.

Task Analysis. For the first three months of the year, that is, for the month numbers less than or equal to three, the rate of charge is the same. For the next three, but less than or equal to six, the rate of charge is the same. The next three months and the last three months are at a similar rate. To determine the charge for taking a bicycle from the shop, we require two inputs: the number of the month in which a request is made for hire and the number of days for which the hire is effective. However, the month number given as input should be validated first and then the number of days for hire should be accepted as input. As the rates for the month numbers are given, the calculation of the charge of hiring after discount, if any, is very simple and is shown in the flowchart for Problem 3.12.

The solution of Problem 3.12 is shown in the following algorithm:

Step 1. REPEAT STEPS 2 THROUGH 9
Step 2. INPUT TO MNO
Step 3. IF MNO = 0
    THEN EXIT
    END-IF
Step 4. IF MNO > 12
    THEN PRINT "INVALID MONTH NUMBER"
    CONTINUE
    END-IF
Step 5. INPUT TO ND
    (Accept no. of days)

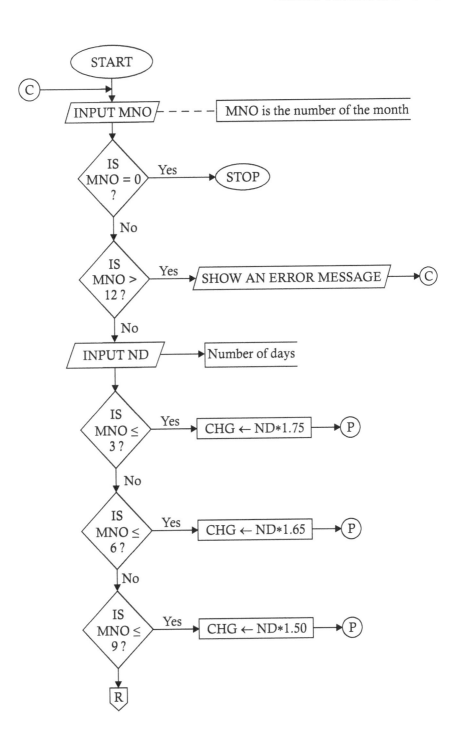

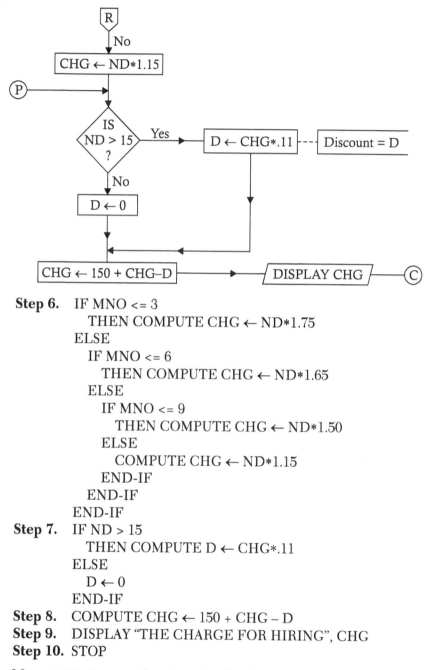

Step 6.   IF MNO <= 3
   THEN COMPUTE CHG ← ND*1.75
   ELSE
    IF MNO <= 6
     THEN COMPUTE CHG ← ND*1.65
    ELSE
     IF MNO <= 9
      THEN COMPUTE CHG ← ND*1.50
     ELSE
      COMPUTE CHG ← ND*1.15
     END-IF
    END-IF
   END-IF
Step 7.   IF ND > 15
   THEN COMPUTE D ← CHG*.11
   ELSE
    D ← 0
   END-IF
Step 8.   COMPUTE CHG ← 150 + CHG – D
Step 9.   DISPLAY "THE CHARGE FOR HIRING", CHG
Step 10. STOP

Problem 3.13. *Draw a flowchart for the following problem to determine the grade. There are 3 tests for 3 different subjects. On the basis of grades in the three subjects, M1, M2, and M3, a grade is awarded to each student as per the following rules:*

a. *If the score in each subject is more than 80, and the total is more than 250, the grade is A +*
b. *If the score in each subject is more than 60, and the total is more than 200, the grade is A*
c. *If the score in any one or more subjects is less than 50, the grade is F*
d. *In all other cases, the grade is B.*

Task Analysis. This problem involves the task of nested decision-making. The inputs required are the grades for the three subjects. In addition, a student identification number may be accepted as input. The procedure will include calculation of the total grades obtained by a student and then comparison of the individual grades and the total grades according to the rules of gradation to determine the grade.

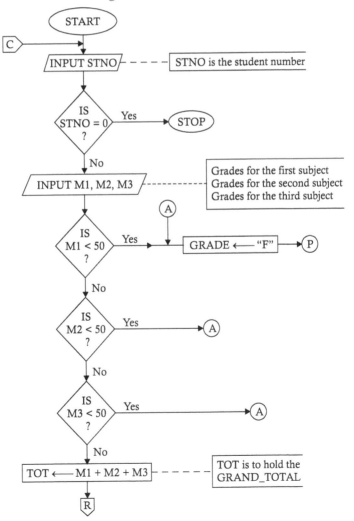

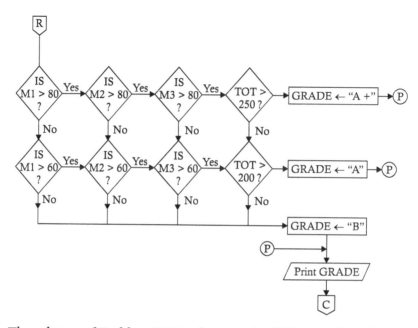

The solution of Problem 3.13 is shown in the following algorithm:

Step 1. FOR EACH STNO DO
Step 2. INPUT TO STNO
Step 3. IF STNO = 0 THEN EXIT
    END-IF
Step 4. INPUT TO M1, M2, M3
Step 5. IF M1 < 50 OR M2 < 50 OR M3 < 50
    THEN GRADE ← "F"
    END-IF
Step 6. COMPUTE TOT ← M1 + M2 + M3
Step 7. IF M1 > 80 AND M2 > 80 AND M3 > 80 AND TOT > 250
    THEN GRADE ← "A+"
    ELSE IF M1 > 60 AND M2 > 60 AND M3 > 60 AND TOT > 200
    THEN GRADE ← "A"
    ELSE
      GRADE ← "B"
    END-IF
    END-IF
Step 8. PRINT GRADE
Step 9. END-FOR
Step 10. STOP

Problem 3.14. *Construct a flowchart to show how to find the product of N natural numbers.*

Task Analysis. The natural numbers are obtained in the same way as we found them earlier. The successive numbers are obtained through the consecutive addition of 1 to the previously obtained number and the product is obtained through consecutive multiplication of the previous product and the newly derived number. This is continued until the number of numbers multiplied equal N.

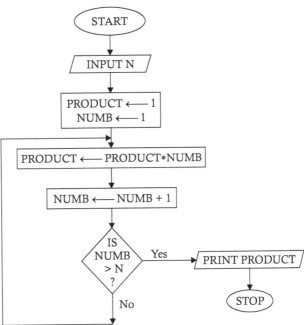

The algorithm showing the solution of Problem 3.14 is given below:

Step 1. INPUT TO N
Step 2. [INITIALIZE VARIABLES REQUIRED]
PRODUCT ← 1, NUMB ← 1
Step 3. REPEAT WHILE NUMB <= N
Step 4. COMPUTE PRODUCT ← PRODUCT*NUMB
[CALCULATE PRODUCT]
Step 5. COMPUTE NUMB ← NUMB + 1
[INCREMENT NUMB]
Step 6. END-WHILE
Step 7. PRINT PRODUCT
Step 8. STOP

Problem 3.15. *Draw a flowchart to show how to find all even natural numbers that are divisible by 7 in a given range.*

Task Analysis. We require two numbers that can serve as boundary values between all the desired numbers to be generated. If a number within the given range is divisible by 7, then it is printed. As the range may include many numbers, each of the numbers need not be accepted as input from the terminal because it will slow down the whole process. We can generate natural numbers one by one based on the lower range given, and then we test the divisibility by 7. A number is said to be divisible by 7 if it leaves no remainder when divided by 7. The input is the numbers forming the lower and the upper ranges between which we test all the numbers, including the numbers forming the ranges. A loop is required to perform the same task of divisibility checking with a newly generated number.

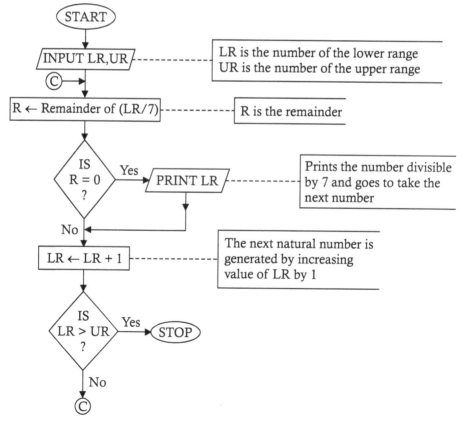

The solution of Problem 3.15 is shown through the following algorithm:

Step 1. INPUT TO LR, UR

Step 2. REPEAT STEPS 3 THROUGH 5 UNTIL
LR > UR
Step 3. COMPUTE R ← REMAINDER OF (LR/7)
Step 4. IF R = 0 THEN PRINT LR END-IF
Step 5. COMPUTE LR ← LR + 1
(INCREASE THE VALUE OF LR)
Step 6. STOP

Problem 3.16. *Construct a flowchart to find the sum of the squares of the first 9 natural numbers that are divisible by 3.*

Task Analysis. The problem requires the natural numbers divisible by 3 to obtain their square values and then to accumulate 9 such consecutive square values as the sum of the values.

Our procedure to obtain the sum should encompass generating natural numbers one by one, testing each for divisibility by 3. If one is found to be divisible, we need to obtain the square of the number to determine the desired sum.

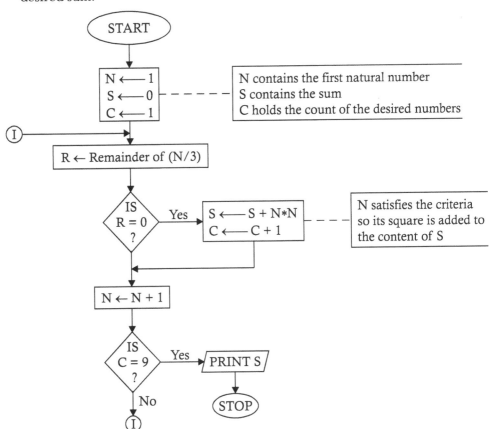

The solution of Problem 3.16 is shown in the following algorithm:

Step 1. [INITIALIZE VARIABLES]
N ← 1
S ← 1
C ← 1
Step 2. REPEAT WHILE C <= 9
Step 3. COMPUTE R ← REMAINDER OF (N/3)
Step 4. IF R = 0
THEN COMPUTE S ← S + N*N
COMPUTE C ← C + 1
END-IF
Step 5. COMPUTE N ← N + 1
Step 6. PRINT S
Step 7. STOP

Problem 3.17. *Construct a flowchart to show how to find the sum of all the numbers that are divisible by P but not divisible by Q within a given range.*

Task Analysis. We are required to test the natural numbers one by one that fall within a given range and are divisible by some given number p, but not divisible by another given number Q. We require four inputs from the user of this procedure: the lower and upper ranges of the numbers to be checked, P and Q. The natural numbers can be generated serially, as done earlier. We have also seen how the divisibility can be checked.

The algorithm of Problem 3.17 is shown below:

Step 1. INPUT TO LR, UR, P, Q
Step 2. [INITIALIZE] N ← LR, S ← 0
Step 3. REPEAT STEPS 4 TO 6 UNTIL N > UR
Step 4. COMPUTE R1 ← N% P
COMPUTE R2 ← N% Q
Step 5. IF R1 = 0 AND R2 NOT = 0
THEN COMPUTE S ← S + N
END-IF
Step 6. COMPUTE N ← N + 1
Step 7. PRINT S
Step 8. STOP

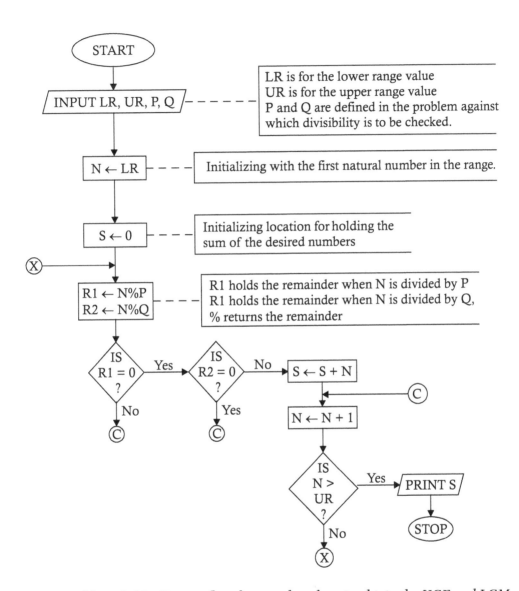

Problem 3.18. *Draw a flowchart to show how to obtain the HCF and LCM of two numbers.*

Task Analysis. We know that HCF (Highest Common Factor) of two numbers is the largest number that can divide the two numbers without leaving any remainder and the LCM (Least Common Multiple) of two numbers is the smaller number that is divisible by both the numbers. The best way to obtain the HCF is the method of division in which one number is divided by another number to see if the remainder is zero. The divisor number is the HCF. If it is other than zero, then the divisor is made the dividend, the remainder is made the divisor, and the division is repeated to obtain the remainder again. This change of dividend and divisor is done repeatedly until we get the divisor that leaves zero as the remainder and the divisor in the last case is the HCF of the given numbers.

The easiest way to find the LCM is to use the relationship between the HCF and LCM. We know that the product of two numbers equals the product of their HCF and LCM. The LCM can be obtained by dividing the product of the given numbers by that HCF. This is shown below:

$$\textbf{LCM} \times \textbf{HCF of two numbers} = \textbf{Product of the two numbers}$$

$$\textbf{LCM of two numbers} = \frac{\textbf{Product of the two numbers}}{\textbf{HCF of the two numbers}}$$

We require two inputs only: the two numbers we use to determine the HCF and LCM. The procedure described above is depicted in the flowchart.

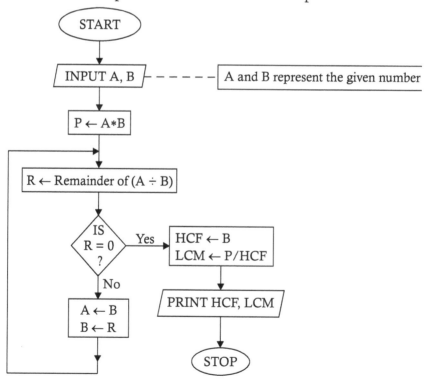

The solution of Problem 3.18 is shown through the following algorithm:

Step 1. INPUT TO A, B
Step 2. COMPUTE P ← A*B
Step 3. [INITIALIZE] R ← 1
Step 4. WHILE R NOT = 0 DO
Step 5. COMPUTE R ← REMAINDER OF (A/B)
Step 6. A ← B
Step 7. B ← R
Step 8. END-WHILE
Step 9. HCF ← A
Step 10. COMPUTE LCM ← P/HCF
Step 11. PRINT "HCF IS", HCF
Step 12. PRINT "LCM IS", LCM
Step 13. STOP

Problem 3.19. *Draw a flowchart to show how the sum of the digits of a given number can be obtained.*

Task Analysis. Observe that a number is stored in a location as integral whole, so its digits cannot be obtained by reading them one by one. To obtain the digits one by one, we can divide the number by 10 to obtain the remainder, and this remainder will always be the last digit of the number. This last digit can be stored in some accumulator. The number can then be replaced with its integral quotient to repeat the previous division; this will return the digit left to the last one that can be added to the content of the accumulator. The procedure can be repeated for obtaining the digits one by one and then to obtain the sum until the dividend is reduced to zero. For example, if the given number is 125, we obtain 5 as remainder when it is divided by 10, which is the 3rd digit of the number. We then replace 125 with 12, as 12 is the integral quotient of 125 divided by 10. When 12 is divided by 10 again, we get 2 as remainder, which is the 2nd digit of the number; we then replace 12 with 1, which is the integral quotient of 12 divided by 10. This 1, when divided by 10 again, leaves 1 as remainder, which is the first digit of the given number. The digits of any given whole number can be obtained serially from the last to the first by using this procedure. Finally, we terminate the procedure when the number after replacement with the integral quotient of the available number divided by 10 becomes zero (here, the integer part of 1/10 = 0). The remainders can be summed up each time it is obtained.

The only input required here is the number for which we want the sum of the digits. This is shown in the following flowchart.

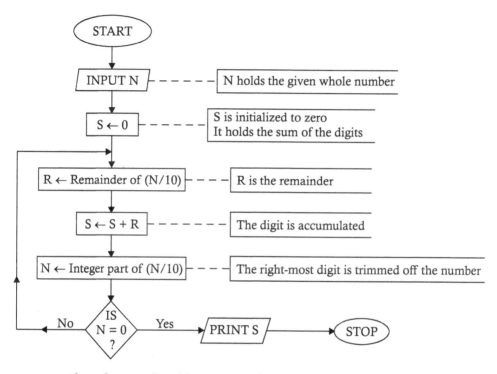

The solution of Problem 3.19 is shown in the following algorithm:

Step 1. INPUT TO N
Step 2. [INITIALIZE] S ← 0
Step 3. REPEAT STEPS 4 THROUGH 6 WHILE N > 0
Step 4. COMPUTE R ← REMAINDER OF (N/10)
(This is to obtain the right-most digit of the number)
Step 5. COMPUTE S ← S + R
Step 6. COMPUTE N ← INTEGER PART OF (N/10)
(This is to get the number in N without the right-most digit)
Step 7. PRINT "THE SUM OF THE DIGITS IS", S
Step 8. STOP

Problem 3.20. *Draw a flowchart to show the logic of obtaining the reversed form of a given whole number.*

Task Analysis. To obtain the reversed form of any given whole number from the last to the first, the digits can be shown one by one without changing the line, which will place the digits in reversed sequence to give the appearance of the number with the digits reversed. To obtain the digits of the numbers one by one, we use identical logic to that of the preceding solution. However, if the leading zeroes in the reversed form are ignored, then an alternative procedure can be used to print the digits of the reversed number. This procedure involves a location initially containing zero; the remainder is added to the value of the location multiplied by 10. The multiplication by 10 changes nothing first and the remainder (*i.e.*, the last digit) is stored there first. If the process of determining the remainder and then adding the remainder to the 10 times of the value of the location is repeated, the last digit is shifted one digit to the left. This continues for the reversed form of the number. Let us illustrate the procedure described using an example. Suppose the given number is 125. Let the location to contain the reversed form contain 0 and let its name be S. Let the name of the location containing 125 be N. The remainder R obtained by dividing N by 10 contains 5 now. If we execute S ← S*10 + R, then the value of R(5) is stored in S. Now, we replace the value of N with the integer part of (N/10), *i.e.*, 12. The remainder R this time becomes 2 and if we execute S ← S*10 + R, S contains 52; we again replace N with integer part of (N/10), *i.e.*, with 1 and take the remainder, which is 1. We get 521 by executing S. S*10 + R is the reversed form of the given number. The procedure is terminated when we get the integer part of (N/10) to be 0. The second procedure is demonstrated in the following flowchart.

The algorithm corresponding to Problem 3.20 is shown below:

Step 1. INPUT TO N
(ACCEPT THE GIVEN NUMBER IN N)

Step 2. [INITIALIZE THE LOCATION TO CONTAIN
THE REVERSED NUMBER]
S ← 0

Step 3. WHILE N > 0 DO
(*i*) COMPUTE R ← REMAINDER (N/10)
[Extract the right-most digit of the number being reversed]
(*ii*) COMPUTE S ← S*10 + R
[Increase the previously reversed integer representation S by a factor 10 and add it to the most recently extracted digit to obtain the current value of S]
(*iii*) COMPUTE N ← integer part of (N/10)
[Use the integer division by 10 to remove the right-most digit from the number being reversed]

Step 4. PRINT "THE REVERSED VALUE OF", N, "IS", S

Step 5. STOP

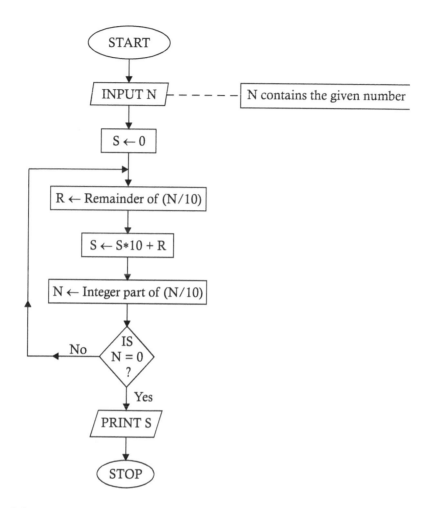

Problem 3.21. *Construct a flowchart to show how the divisors of a given number can be obtained.*

Task Analysis. A number is called a divisor of another number if the division of the latter by the former leaves zero as the remainder. Usually, the whole numbers starting from 1 are used as divisors. Divisors are also known as factors of the number. To obtain all the divisors of a number, we need to start testing from 1 until we reach the half of the number after which only the number itself remains as its divisor.

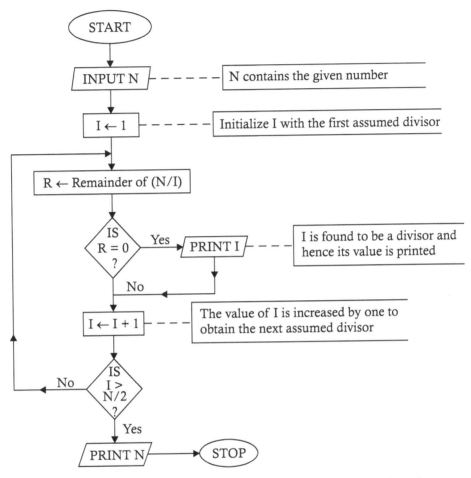

The solution to Problem 3.21 is shown in the following algorithm:

Step 1. INPUT TO N
[ACCEPT the number the divisors of which are to be obtained and store it in N]

Step 2. [Set the initial value of the divisor]
I ← 1

Step 3. While I <= integer part of (N/2) DO
(*i*) COMPUTE R ← REMAINDER OF (N/I)
(*ii*) IF R = 0
THEN PRINT I
END-IF
(*iii*) COMPUTE I ← I + 1
[Increment the value of the divisor]

Step 4. PRINT N
[This prints the last divisor]
Step 5. STOP

Problem 3.22. *Construct a flowchart to show how to determine whether a given number is a perfect number.*

Task Analysis. A number is said to be a perfect number if the sum of its divisors (except itself) equals the number. To draw the desired conclusion about the given number, we require the divisors of the number and the sum of the divisors. The preceding procedure describes and shows how to obtain the divisors.

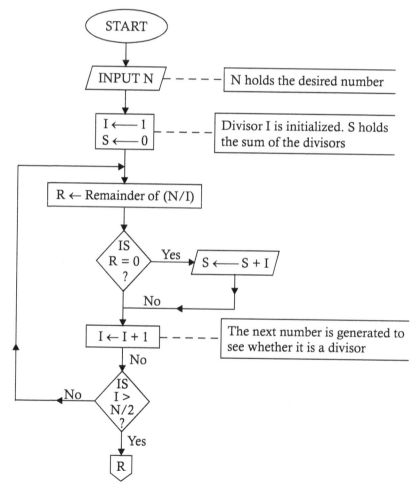

The following algorithm depicts the steps leading to the solution for Problem 3.22:

Step 1. INPUT TO N
[ACCEPT THE DESIRED INTEGER AND STORE IT]

Step 2. [INITIALIZE THE DIVISOR LOCATION I & THE LOCATION S TO CONTAIN THE SUM OF THE DIVISORS]

Step 3. WHILE I <= Integer part of (N/2) DO
(*i*) COMPUTE R ← REMAINDER OF (N/I)
(*ii*) IF R = 0
    THEN COMPUTE S ← S + I
    [ACCUMULATE THE DIVISOR OBTAINED]
    END-IF
(*iii*) COMPUTE I ← I + 1
    [INCREMENT I TO SEE WHETHER IT IS THE NEXT DIVISOR]

Step 4. If S = N
    THEN PRINT N, "IS A PERFECT NUMBER."
    ELSE
    PRINT N, "IS NOT A PERFECT NUMBER."
    END-IF

Step 5. STOP

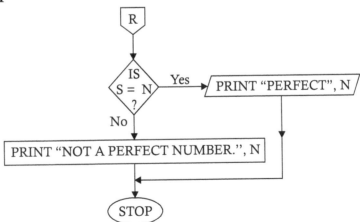

Problem 3.23. *Construct a flowchart to show how you can decide if a given number is prime or not.*

Task Analysis. We know that a number can be called a prime number if, and only if, it has no divisor or factor except itself and unity, *i.e.*, 1. In order to declare that a number is a prime number, we need to prove that the number is not divisible by any number starting from 2 to the half of the given number because we have already seen that if a number has some divisor at all, it must lie within the half of the number. A better, more efficient strategy is to limit the checking within the integer part of the square root of the number. For example, to check if the number 97 is a prime number, we need check whether there exists some divisor of 97 within 2 to 48 (both inclusive). This checking can be done from 2 to 9, because 9 is the integer part of the square root of 97. The number of checking is decreased to a large extent. The divisors can be generated automatically by changing the value of a variable location. Assuming that the procedure for determining the square root of a number is available, we can draw the flowchart for the task.

The following algorithm shows the steps leading to the solution for Problem 3.23:

Step 1. INPUT TO N
[ACCEPT THE NUMBER WHOSE SQUARE ROOT IS TO BE FOUND]

Step 2. COMPUTE SR ← SQUARE ROOT OF (N)

Step 3. [INITIALIZE] I ← 2, FLAG ← 0
[FLAG contains the divisibility status of the number]

Step 4. WHILE I <= SR DO
(*i*) COMPUTE R ← REMAINDER OF (N/I)
(*ii*) IF R = 0
THEN FLAG ← 1
EXIT
END-IF
(*iii*) COMPUTE I ← I + 1
(Increment I to obtain the next divisor]

Step 5. IF   FLAG = 0
THEN PRINT "It is a prime number."
ELSE
PRINT "It is not a prime number."
END-IF

Step 6. STOP

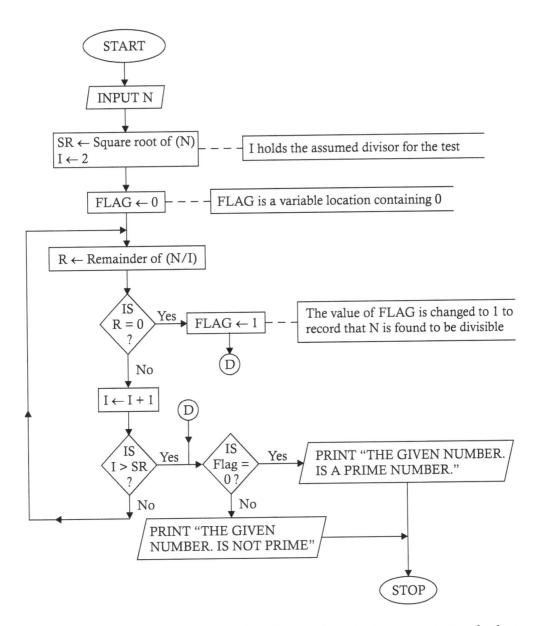

Problem 3.24. *Construct a flowchart to show the logic of printing the first N Fibonacci numbers. Fibonacci numbers are obtained from the relationship* $t_i = t_{i-1} + t_{i-2}$, *i = 2 to n where* $t_o = 0$, $t_1 = 1$.

Task Analysis. Any Fibonacci number can be obtained by taking the sum of the preceding two numbers. For example, the third Fibonacci number is obtained by taking the sum of the first two, *i.e.*, 0 + 1 = 1; the fourth Fibonacci number is obtained by taking the sum of the 2nd and the 3rd number, *i.e.*, 1 + 1 = 2. Hence, a simple expression of the form C = A + B can be built and used to generate the Fibonacci numbers, where A and B will initially represent the first two Fibonacci numbers and C the 3rd one. Having obtained the 3rd Fibonacci number, we can assign the value of B to A and that of C to B to get the 2nd and the 3rd Fibonacci numbers in A and B, and then, using the expression (*i.e.*, C = A + B), we can derive the fourth Fibonacci number. This procedure of assigning the value of B to A and C to B to get the next Fibonacci number can be repeated any number times until the desired numbers are obtained. A counter may be maintained to count the numbers printed. This is shown in the flowchart.

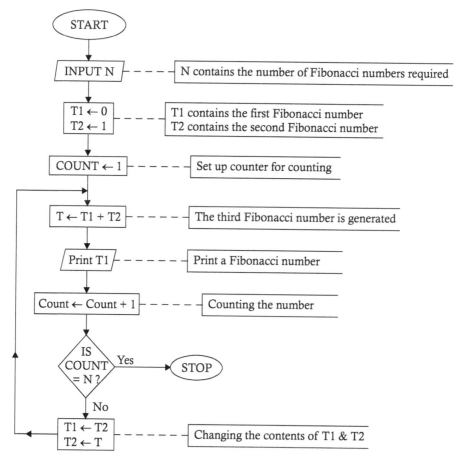

The algorithm below shows the solution of Problem 3.24.

Step 1. INPUT TO N
[Establish N, the number of FIBONACCI NUMBERS to be generated]

Step 2. [INITIALIZE VARIABLES WITH THE FIRST TWO FIBONACCI NUMBERS]
T1 ← 0,   T2 ← 1

Step 3. [INITIALIZE THE COUNTER VARIABLE]
COUNT ← 0

Step 4.   WHILE COUNT <= N
(*i*) COMPUTE T ← T1 + T2
(*ii*) PRINT T1
(*iii*) COMPUTE COUNT ← COUNT + 1
(*iv*) T1 ← T2
(*v*) T2 ← T

Step 5. STOP

Problem 3.25. *Construct a flowchart to show if a given year is leap year.*

Task Analysis. A given year is said to be a leap year if it is a non-century year (*i.e.*, not like 1900, 1800, or 1600) and it is divisible by 4. In case it is a century year, then it must be divisible by 400 to be a leap year. To determine whether a given year is a leap year, we determine whether the year is divisible by 4 but not by 100 or if it is divisible by 400. The divisibility is tested again in the way as we have seen earlier, *i.e.*, by checking whether the remainder in the division process is zero or not.

Step 1. Y ← 1
Step 2. REPEAT STEPS 2 TO 8 UNTIL Y = 0
Step 3. INPUT TO Y
[ACCEPT YEAR TO BE TESTED AND STORE IT IN Y]
Step 4. IF Y = 0
THEN EXIT
END-IF
Step 5. COMPUTE R1 ← REMAINDER OF (Y/400)
Step 6. IF R1 = 0
THEN PRINT "THE GIVEN YEAR IS A LEAP YEAR"
END-IF

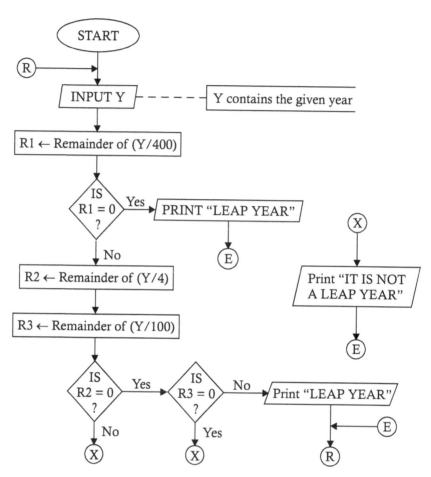

Step 7. COMPUTE R2 ← REMAINDER OF (Y/4)
Step 8. COMPUTE R3 ← REMAINDER OF (Y/100)
Step 9. IF R2 = 0 AND R3 NOT = 0
    THEN PRINT "THE GIVEN YEAR IS A LEAP YEAR"
    ELSE
    PRINT "THE GIVEN YEAR IS NOT A LEAP YEAR"
    END-IF
Step 10. STOP

Problem 3.26. *Construct a flowchart to show how the square root of a positive number is determined.*

Task Analysis. The square root of a number can be obtained by using the Newton Raphson Method. In this method, the square root of any positive number is initially set to 1. Then the absolute value of the difference between the square of the assumed square root and the given number is obtained. This value is then compared with some predefined small positive number. This small positive number is set in such a way that an error of magnitude less than that is made acceptable. If the difference is less than the small positive number, the assumed square root is used as the desired square root. For perfect squares, this difference becomes zero; for others, this difference is usually found to be of magnitude less than .01, .001, or .0001, depending upon the precision required. If the difference is greater than or equal to the small positive number like .001 or .0001, then the assumed value is increased to have a better guess by using the formula

$$\left(\text{Guessed Value} + \frac{\text{Number}}{\text{Guessed Value}} \right) \Big/ 2$$

The procedure is repeated until we get a guessed value satisfying the condition specified. Algorithmically, we can express the procedure as shown below.

Let X be the number whose square root is to be obtained.

1. Set Guess to 1.
2. If | GUESS*GUESS-X | < Epsilon
Then go to step 5
(Epsilon is a predefined small positive number)

3. Set Guess to $\left(\text{Guess} + \dfrac{X}{\text{Guess}} \right) \Big/ 2$

4. Go to Step 2
5. Guess is the square root of X.
The flowchart corresponding to Problem 3.26 is shown in next page.
The algorithm for the solution of Problem 3.26 is given below:

Step 1. INPUT TO X
Step 2. [INITIALIZE] GUESS ← 1, EPSILON ← .001
Step 3. WHILE absolute value of (GUESS*GUESS – X) <= EPSILON DO

$$\text{COMPUTE GUESS} \leftarrow \left(\text{GUESS} + \frac{X}{\text{GUESS}} \right) \Big/ 2$$

Step 4. PRINT "THE SQUARE ROOT IS", GUESS
Step 5. STOP

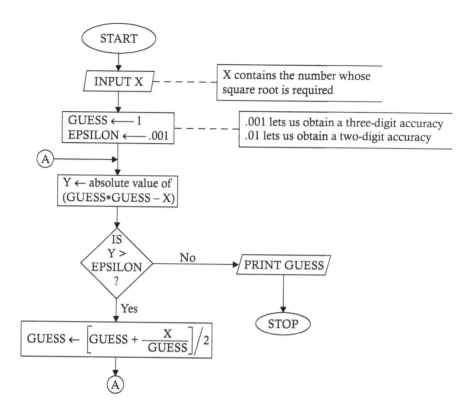

Problem 3.27. *The registration charge for a parcel is determined according to the following rules:*

> *For the 1st 10 oz., the charge is $12.75;*
> *For the next every 8 oz. (or part thereof), the charge is $11.25.*
> *Draw a flowchart to show how the registration charge is determined.*

Task Analysis. Note that the input required here is the weight of the parcel to be registered. The calculation of the charge requires determining whether the weight lies is 10 oz. or less. If not, then the excess weight beyond 10 oz. is computed and the number of 8 ounce intervals for the excess weight is obtained for which the charge is calculated at $ 11.25 per interval. The number of 8 ounce intervals is computed by dividing the excess weight by 8. If the division leaves no remainder, then the quotient will be the number of intervals. If the division leaves some other remainder, then the number of intervals will be the quotient plus 1. The calculation of the number of intervals can, however, be done by using the following formula also: Number of intervals = integer part of (Excess Weight – 1)/8 + 1.

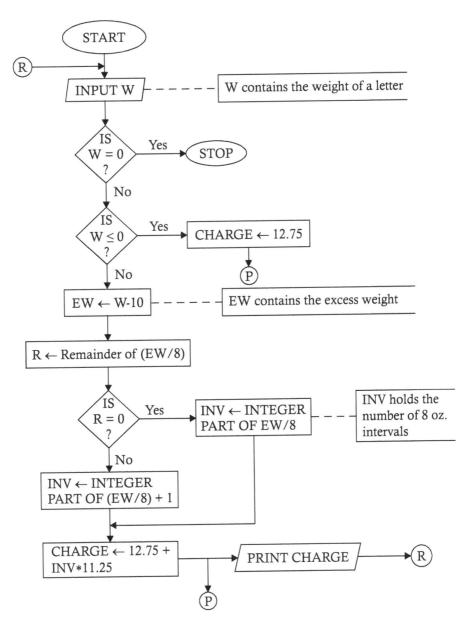

Step 1. REPEAT STEPS 2 THROUGH 6

Step 2. INPUT TO W

Step 3. IF W = 0

   THEN EXIT

   END-IF

Step 4.   IF W <= 10
           THEN CHARGE ← 12.75
       ELSE
         COMPUTE EW ← W – 10
         COMPUTE R ← REMAINDER OF (EW/8)
         IF R = 0
           THEN COMPUTE INV ← Integer part of (EW/8)
         ELSE
           COMPUTE INV ← Integer part of (EW/8) + 1
             END-IF
       END-IF
Step 5.   COMPUTE CHARGE ← 12.75 + INV*11.25
Step 6.   PRINT "THE CHARGE IS $", CHARGE
       END-REPEAT
Step 7.   STOP

Problem 3.28. *The charge for luggage on railways is calculated as shown below:*

For the first 40 kg. of weight, the charge is fixed at $5.75. For every additional 18 kg. (or part thereof), the charge is calculated at the rate of $ 3.88. If the total weight is less than 500 g, for weight beyond 500 kg., the charge is calculated at the rate of $ 0.67 per kg. Develop a flowchart that will show the logic for calculating the charge of transporting a piece of luggage.

Task Analysis. This problem is an extended form of the preceding problem. The logic of the calculation will be of the same nature except that the calculation here will involve one of the three ways. First, we check whether the weight is less than 40 kgs. If so, the determination of the charge is straightforward and needs no calculation. Next, we need to check whether it is less than 500 kgs. If it is under 500 kgs but more than 40 kgs, we have to calculate the number of 18-kg intervals in the same way as we explained in the preceding solution. If the weight is greater than 500 kg, then we have to calculate the excess weight beyond 500 kgs and number of intervals for the weights less than 500 (but greater than 40 kg). Here, we shall use the formula discussed in the preceding solution. The solution to Problem 3.28 in the form of flowchart is shown in next page:

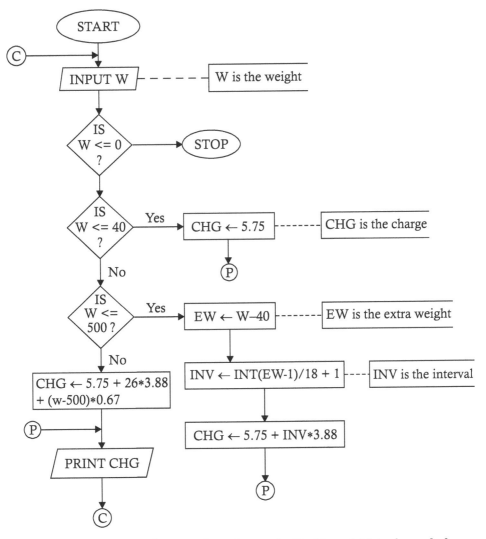

The algorithm showing the solution for Problem 3.28 is shown below:

Step 1. REPEAT STEPS 2 THROUGH 5 UNTIL USER SIGNALS 'EXIT'

Step 2. INPUT TO W
(Accept the weight of the luggage and store it in W)

Step 3. IF W <= 0
    THEN EXIT
END-IF

Step 4. IF W <= 40
    THEN CHG ← 5.75
    ELSE IF W <= 500
        THEN COMPUTE EW ← W – 40

        COMPUTE INV ← Integer part of $\left(\dfrac{EW-1}{18}\right)+1$

        COMPUTE CHG ← 5.75 + INV*3.88
        ELSE
        COMPUTE CHG ← 5.75 + 26*3.88 + (W – 500)*0.67
        END-IF
    END-IF
Step 5. PRINT "THE CHARGE IS $", CHG
Step 6. STOP

Problem 3.29. *Construct a flowchart for obtaining the sum of a given number of terms (N) for a given value of x in the following mathematical series:*

$$X + X^2/2 + X^3/3 + \ldots\ldots upto\ N\ terms.$$

Task Analysis. We need to know the values of two unknown quantities as input: the value of X and that of N, the number of terms. We must find a general expression from which we can identify different terms. The expression X/I yields different terms for different values of I from 1 to N. We can evaluate the expression for some given value of X and the obtained value can be stored in some location, say S, that initially contains 0. Successive addition of the evaluated values for all the terms to the content of S will give us the desired sum. This is shown in the flowchart for Problem 3.29.

The algorithm leading to the solution of Problem 3.29 is shown below:

Step 1. REPEAT STEPS 2 THROUGH 10 WHILE USER LIKES
Step 2. INPUT TO X
    [ACCEPT THE VALUE OF THE UNKNOWN X FROM THE TERMINAL AND STORE IT IN X]
Step 3. IF X <= 0
    THEN STOP
    END-IF
Step 4. INPUT TO N
    [ACCEPT THE NUMBER OF TERMS TO BE ADDED AND STORE IT IN N]

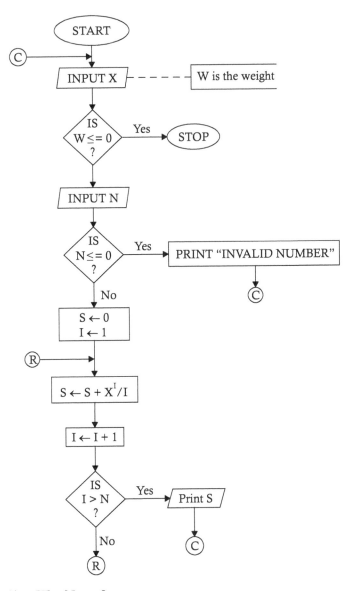

Step 5. IF   N <= 0
THEN PRINT "INVALID NUMBER"
CONTINUE FROM STEP 2
END-IF

Step 6. [INITIALIZE REQUIRED LOCATIONS]
$S \leftarrow 0, I \leftarrow 1$

Step 7. WHILE I <= N REPEAT   STEPS 8 AND 9
Step 8. [PERFORM ADDITION]

$$\text{COMPUTE } S \leftarrow S + \frac{X^I}{I}$$

Step 9. COMPUTE I ← I + 1
Step 10. PRINT "THE SUM IS", S
Step 11. STOP

Problem 3.30. *The difference between two consecutive gas meter readings gives the amount of gas used in cubic feet. The gas charge is calculated using the following rules.*

No. of therms consumed	Rate/therm (in $.)
<= 75	1.05
> 75 but <= 150	1.25
> 150 but <= 250	1.50
> 250	2.25

The number of therms consumed is calculated by multiplying the amount of gas used by 1.06748. A meter rent of $15 is also charged with each bill. The meters show 5-digit readings. Develop a program to print the gas bill for consumers.

Task Analysis. The inputs required here are two consecutive meter readings. The difference between the readings will generally give us the amount of gas used, except in the extreme cases in which the previous reading becomes greater than the present reading. This extreme case occurs because the 5 digit meter resets when it reaches the reading of 100,000 (initially, the meter shows 00000 and it increases as the gas is consumed up to the largest value 99,999, after which one more unit of consumption will reset the meter because the meter does not possess the capacity to show 100,000). When the difference is obtained, it can be multiplied by 1.06748 to derive the number of therms consumed and then the calculation of the charge becomes straightforward.

The algorithm leading to the solution of Problem 3.30 is shown below:

Step 1. [INITIALIZE] CHOICE ← "Y"
Step 2. REPEAT STEPS 3 THROUGH 10 UNTIL CHOICE = "E"
Step 3. INPUT PVR, PRR
Step 4. IF PVR > PRR
    THEN COMPUTE D ← (100000 – PVR) + PRR
    ELSE COMPUTE D ← PRR – PVR
    END-IF
Step 5. COMPUTE TH ← D*1.06748

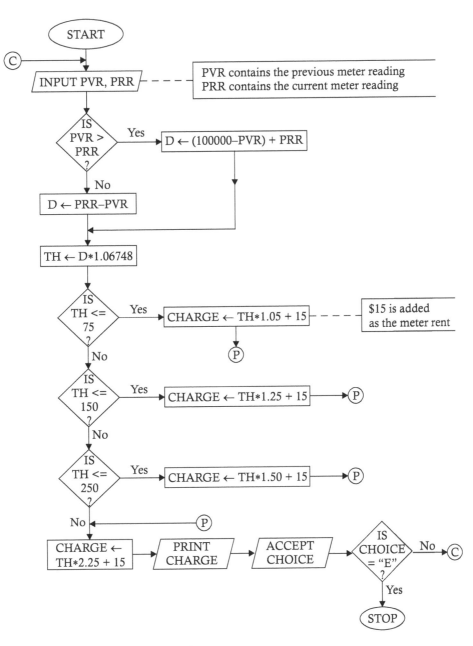

Step 6. IF TH <= 75
       THEN COMPUTE CHARGE ← TH*1.05 + 15
    ELSE IF TH <= 150
       THEN COMPUTE CHARGE ← TH*1.25 + 15

```
          ELSE IF TH <= 250
              THEN COMPUTE CHARGE ← TH*1.50 + 15
          ELSE COMPUTE CHARGE ← TH*2.25 + 15
              END-IF
          END-IF
      END-IF
```
Step 7. PRINT "THE CHARGE IS", CHARGE
Step 8. PRINT "TO TERMINATE ENTER 'E,' ELSE PRESS ANY
OTHER KEY"
Step 9. ACCEPT CHOICE
Step 10. IF CHOICE = "E" THEN EXIT
END-IF
Step 11. STOP

Problem 3.31. *Develop a flowchart to show how the sum of the following series can be obtained:*

$$X - \frac{X^3}{3} + \frac{X^5}{5} - \frac{X^7}{7} + \frac{X^9}{9} \mp \dots\dots up\ to\ n\ terms$$

Task Analysis. The inputs required are X and N. The general expression for any term I can be given by $t_1 = \dfrac{X}{2I-1}$ for I = 1 to N. The flowchart will be same as that for the next problem except that the statement $S \leftarrow S + \dfrac{X^I}{I}$ is replaced with

$$S \leftarrow S + X \frac{2I-1}{2I-1}$$

Problem 3.32. *Develop a flowchart to show how to find out the sum of the following mathematical series:*

$$X - \frac{1}{2}X^3 + \frac{1}{2}\cdot\frac{3}{4}X^5 - \frac{1}{2}\cdot\frac{3}{4}\cdot\frac{5}{6}X^7 + \dots\dots up\ to\ n\ terms$$

Task Analysis. The inputs required here are X and N. The coefficients in this series bear a relationship with each other. The coefficient of the 2nd term is $\dfrac{1}{2}$, that of the 3rd term is $\dfrac{1}{2}\cdot\dfrac{3}{4}$, and that of the 4th term is $\dfrac{1}{2}\cdot\dfrac{3}{4}\cdot\dfrac{5}{6}$. We observe that each coefficient is a result of evaluating an expression of the form $\dfrac{2I-1}{2I}$ for $I = 1, 2 \ldots\ldots$, an expression that generates an odd number in the numerator and an even number in the denominator. For $I = 1$, the coefficient is 1/2 if it is stored somewhere and it is multiplied by the value of the expression next time for $I = 2$, we get the 3rd coefficient; that is, we evaluate an expression of the form $C * (2I - 1)/2I$ for $C = 1$ initially. The successive values of I from 1 to $n - 1$ will give the coefficients from the 2nd to the nth term. Again, if we take $C = -C * (2I - 1)/2I$, we get the coefficients with sign positive or negative. Now, multiplying the expression by X^{2I+1} for different values of I, we get the successive terms, except for the 1st term. Now, if we initialize S with the value of X and add the terms evaluated successively to the current value of S, we get the desired sum of the series. The logic is shown in the flowchart.

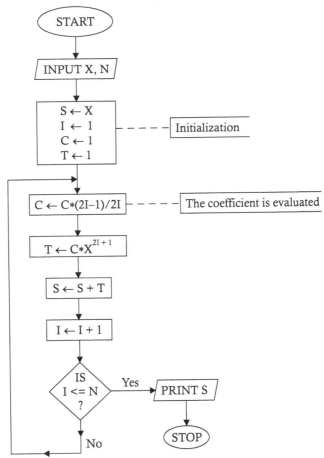

The algorithm leading to the solution of Problem 3.32 is as follows:

Step 1. PRINT "ENTER VALUE OF X"
Step 2. INPUT TO X
Step 3. PRINT "ENTER NUMBER OF TERMS TO ADD"
Step 4. INPUT TO N
Step 5. [INITIALIZE SUM ACCUMULATOR, LOOP VARIABLE, COEFFICIENT, & TERM VARIABLE]
$S \leftarrow X, I \leftarrow 1, C \leftarrow 1, T \leftarrow 1$
Step 6. REPEAT WHILE I $<=$ N
    (a) COMPUTE $C \leftarrow -C*(2*I - 1)/(2*I)$
      [Obtain the Ith COEFFICIENT]
    (b) COMPUTE $T \leftarrow C*X^{2*I+1}$
      [Obtain the Ith term]
    (c) COMPUTE $S \leftarrow S + T$
      [Obtain the sum of the Ith term]
    (d) COMPUTE $I \leftarrow I + 1$
      [Increment the loop counter]
Step 7. PRINT "THE SUM IS", S
Step 8. STOP

Problem 3.33. *Develop a flowchart to show how to evaluate the following series:*

$$X - \frac{X^3}{3!} + \frac{X^5}{5!} - \frac{X^7}{7!} + \ldots\ldots\ldots up\ to\ N\ terms.$$

Task Analysis. To evaluate the series, we need two inputs: the values of X and N. The different expressions of X can be generated easily. The expression X^{2I+1} will yield different expressions of X for I = 1 to N. The generation of coefficients can be done by evaluating the expression (2I)(2I + 1) for different values of I from 1 to N – 1, and then through cumulative multiplication, as shown in the preceding flowchart. The steps of the calculations for Problem 3.33 are depicted in the following flowchart within an outer loop.

The algorithm leading to the solution of Problem 3.33 is given below:

Step 1. [INITIALIZE LOOP VARIABLE]
OPTION $\leftarrow$ "Y"
Step 2. REPEAT STEPS 3 THROUGH 8 WHILE OPTION = "Y"
Step 3. PRINT "ENTER VALUE FOR X"

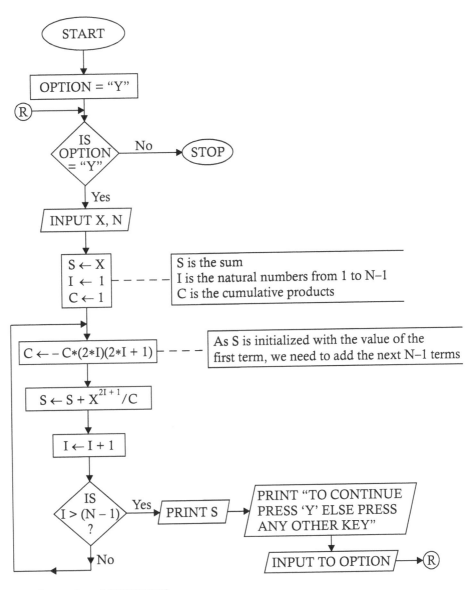

Step 4. ACCEPT X
Step 5. PRINT "ENTER THE NUMBER OF TERMS TO
BE ADDED"
Step 6. ACCEPT N
Step 7. [INITIALIZE SUM ACCUMULATOR, LOOP VARIABLE,
& COEFFICIENT VARIABLE]
$S \leftarrow X, I \leftarrow 1, C \leftarrow 1$

Step 8. WHILE I <= N DO
   (*a*) COMPUTE C ← – C*(2*I)*(2*I + 1)
      [Obtain the (I + 1)th COEFFICIENT]
   (*b*) COMPUTE S ← S + X$^{(2*I + 1)}$/C
      [Obtain sum of the (I + 1)th term]
   (*c*) COMPUTE I ← I + 1
      [INCREMENT LOOP VARIABLE]
Step 9. PRINT "THE SUM IS", S
Step 10. STOP

Problem 3.34. *Construct a flowchart to find out the sum of first N terms of the following series.* 5 + 55 + 555 + 5555 + ... *up to N terms.*

Task Analysis. The only input required is the number of terms to be added. The different terms can be obtained by evaluating the expression T = T*10 + 5, with 0 as the initial value of T.

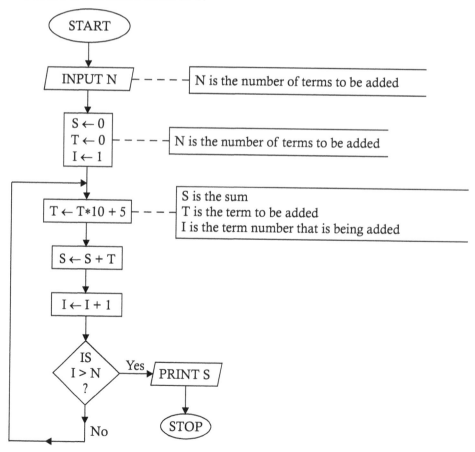

The algorithm corresponding to the solution of Problem 3.34 is shown below:

Step 1. PRINT "ENTER THE NUMBER OF TERMS TO ADD"
Step 2. ACCEPT N
Step 3. [INITIALIZE SUM ACCUMULATOR, TERM VARIABLE, & LOOP VARIABLE]
$S \leftarrow 0, T \leftarrow 0, I \leftarrow 1$
Step 4. WHILE I <= N DO
(a) COMPUTE $T \leftarrow T*10 + 5$
[Obtain the term to be added]
(b) COMPUTE $S \leftarrow S + T$
[Accumulate the term]
(c) COMPUTE $I \leftarrow I + 1$
[Increment counter]
END-DO
Step 5. PRINT "THE SUM IS", S
Step 6. STOP

Problem 3.35. *Develop a flowchart to show how to find all the perfect numbers under 10,000.*

Task Analysis. We saw earlier how to determine perfect numbers. We need to test all the natural numbers within 10,000 and print a number in the range whenever it is found to be perfect. As we know that the first perfect number is 6, we can start testing numbers from 6. The solution of this problem will require a nested loop. The outer loop generates the numbers one by one, and the inner loop finds the sum of the divisors of each of the generated numbers. Having obtained the sum of the divisors, the number under consideration is then compared with the resulting sum to decide whether the taken number is perfect or not. If it is a perfect number, the task is to print it and then to transfer the control back to the process of number generation to test the next one unless the highest limit is reached.

The steps of the solution to Problem 3.35 are depicted in the following flowchart.

The algorithm corresponding to Problem 3.35 is shown below:

Step 1. [INITIALIZE N] $N \leftarrow 6$
Step 2. REPEAT STEPS 3 TO 10 FOR N = 6 TO 10000
Step 3. [INITIALIZE S FOR HOLDING THE SUM OF DIVISORS AND I FOR DIVISOR BEING TAKEN]
$S \leftarrow 0$
$I \leftarrow 1$

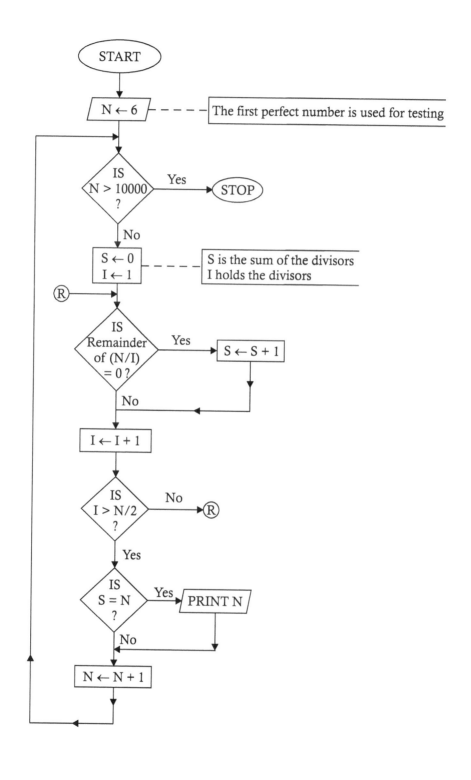

Step 4. REPEAT STEPS 5 TO 8 WHILE I <= N/2

Step 5. [OBTAIN THE INTEGER QUOTIENT] Q ← N/I

Step 6. [OBTAIN THE REMAINDER] R ← N – Q*I

Step 7. IF R = 0 [*i.e.*, IF N IS DIVISIBLE BY I]
      THEN S ← S + R
      END-IF

Step 8. [INCREMENT I TO TAKE THE NEXT NUMBER AS DIVISOR]
      I ← I + 1

Step 9. IF   S = N THEN PRINT N

Step 10. [INCREMENT N TO TAKE THE NEXT NUMBER]
      N ← N + 1

Step 11. STOP

Problem 3.36. *Develop a flowchart to show how to determine all the 3-digit Armstrong numbers. A number is called an Armstrong number if the sum of the values of the digits each raised to the power equal to the number of digits in the number equals the number. For example, 153 is an Armstrong number, because $153 = 1^3 + 5^3 + 3^3$.*

Task Analysis. We need to test all the 3-digit numbers, from 100 to 999. A loop is required to generate the numbers to be tested one by one. Next, each of the generated numbers is to be broken down into its component digits to obtain the sum of the cube of each. We saw earlier that digits making a number can be separated if the number is divided by 10 and the remainder is obtained repeatedly each time by replacing the number with the integer part of the quotient. An iteration process is required for each of the numbers. Hence, in the solution of this problem too we have to use a nested loop. The steps of the computable process for Problem 3.36 are depicted in the flowchart.

This algorithm finds all 3-digit Armstrong numbers.

Step 1. [INITIALIZE N WITH THE FIRST 3-DIGIT NUMBER]
      N ← 100

Step 2. REPEAT STEPS 3 THROUGH 10 UNTIL N > 999

Step 3. [INITIALIZE S, WHICH HOLDS THE SUM OR THE CUBES]
      S ← 0

Step 4. M ← N [THIS IS TO MAKE A COPY OR N]

Step 5. REPEAT STEP 6 THROUGH STEP 8 WHILE M > 0

Step 6. COMPUTE REM ← REMAINDER OF (M/10)

Step 7. COMPUTE S ← S + REM*REM*REM

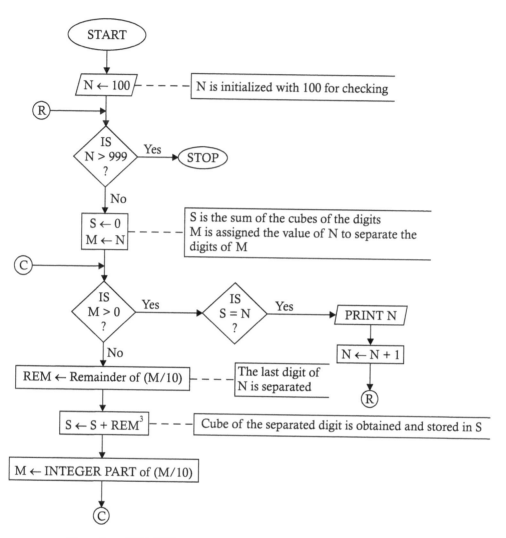

Step 8. COMPUTE M ← INTEGER PART OF (M/10)
Step 9. IF   S = N
          THEN PRINT N
          END-IF
Step 10. [INCREMENT N TO TAKE THE NEXT NUMBER]
          COMPUTE N ← N + 1
          END-REPEAT
Step 11. END

Problem 3.37. *Some three-digit numbers show the property that the sum of the factorials of the digits equals the numbers, for example, 145 = 1 ! + 4 ! + 5 !. Develop a flowchart to show how to determine all such numbers.*

Task Analysis. In this problem, too, we do not require any input from the terminal because we need to test all the three-digit numbers as in the preceding problem that can be generated serially. This solution requires a nested loop. The determination of the factorial was shown earlier. Here, the process should be repeated for each of the digits. The following flowchart shows the steps of the solution.

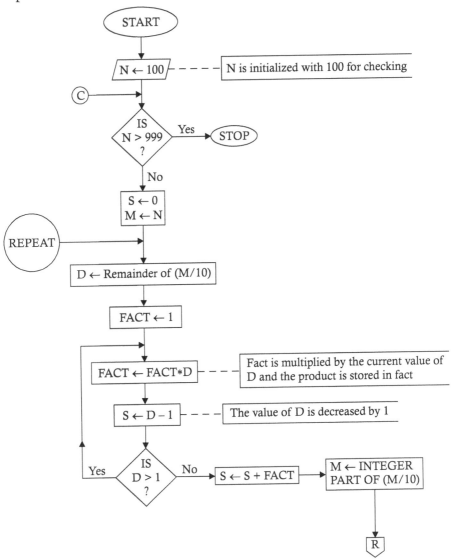

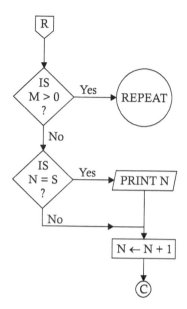

This algorithm is to find out all the 3-digit numbers for which the sum of the factorials of the digits equals the number.

Step 1. [INITIALIZE N WITH THE FIRST 3-DIGIT NUMBER]
N ← 100

Step 2. REPEAT STEPS 3 THROUGH STEP 15 UNTIL N > 999

Step 3. [INITIALIZE S, WHICH HOLDS THE SUM OR THE CUBES]
S ← 0

Step 4. [MAKE A COPY OF N] M ← N

Step 5. REPEAT STEP 6 THROUGH STEP 13 WHILE M > 0

Step 6. COMPUTE D ← REMAINDER OF (M/10)

Step 7. [INITIALIZE] FACT ← 1

Step 8. REPEAT WHILE D > 1

Step 9. COMPUTE FACT ← FACT*D

Step 10. COMPUTE D ← D – 1   [DECREMENT D]

Step 11. END-WHILE

Step 12. COMPUTE S ← S + FACT

Step 13. COMPUTE M ← INTEGER PART OF (M/10)

Step 14. IF   N = S
THEN PRINT N
END-IF

Step 15. [INCREMENT N TO TAKE THE NEXT 3-DIGIT NUMBER]
COMPUTE N ← N + 1

Step 16. END

Problem 3.38. *Some two-digit numbers have the property that the sum of the squares of the numbers equals the sum of the squares of the numbers with reversed digits (for example, $48^2 + 52^2 + 63^2 = 84^2 + 25^2 + 36^2$). Construct a flowchart to show how to determine all such two-digit numbers.*

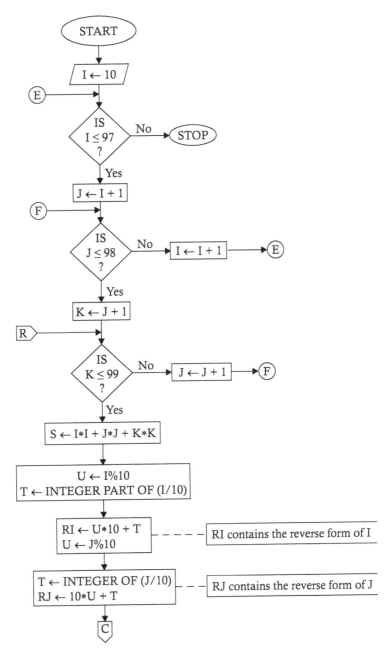

Task Analysis. The solution of this problem requires the checking of all two-digit triplets such that the triplet satisfies the specified property with no number repeated. The repetition of a number can be prevented by establishing three nested loops. The first loop generates numbers from 10 to 97. The next inner loop generates the numbers from 11 to 98 and the next inner loop generates the numbers from 12 to 99 such that the first triplet to be tested is 10, 11, 12 and the next triplet is 10.11, 13. The next task is to obtain the sum of the squares of the numbers with the digits reversed. To obtain a number with the digits reversed, we separate the digits of the unit's place and that of the ten's place. Then we use the formula: the digit of the unit's place * 10 + digit of the ten's place.

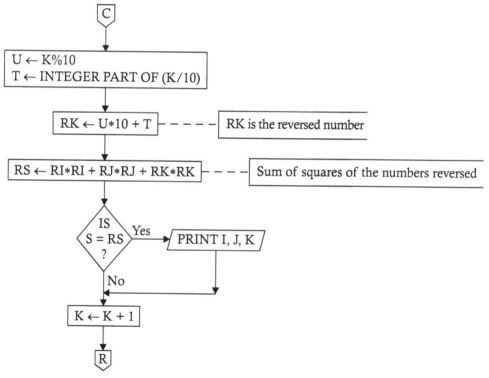

The algorithm corresponding to Problem 3.38 is as follows.:

Step 1. [Initialize the Ist loop variable]
$\quad$ I ← 10
Step 2. REPEAT STEPS 3 TO 19 WHILE I <= 97
Step 3. [Initialize the 2nd loop variable]
$\quad$ J ← I + 1

Step 4. REPEAT STEPS 5 TO 18 WHILE J <= 98

Step 5. [Initialize the 3rd loop variable]

K ← J + 1

Step 6. REPEAT STEPS 7 TO 17 WHILE K <= 99

Step 7. [CALCULATE SUM OF THE SQUARES OF THE 1ST 3 NUMBERS REPRESENTED BY THE LOOP VARIABLES]

Step 8. COMPUTE S ← $I^2 + J^2 + K^2$

Step 9. [SEPARATE THE DIGITS OF THE UNIT'S & TEN'S PLACE OF I]

(*a*) COMPUTE U ← I% 10 [DIVIDE I BY 10 & COLLECT THE REMAINDER]

(*b*) COMPUTE T ← Integer part of (I/10)

Step 10. [Obtain the reversed form of I] COMPUTE RI ← U*10 + T

Step 11. [SEPARATE THE DIGITS OF UNIT'S & TEN'S PLACE OF J]

(*a*) COMPUTE U ← J% 10

(*b*) COMPUTE T ← Integer part of (J/10)

Step 12. [Obtain the reversed form of J] RJ ← U*10 + T

Step 13. [SEPARATE THE DIGITS OF UNIT'S & TEN'S PLACE OF K]

(*a*) COMPUTE U ← K%10

(*b*) COMPUTE T ← Integer part of (K/10)

Step 14. COMPUTE RK ← U × 10 + T [REVERSED FORM OF K]

Step 15. [Obtain the sum of the squares of the reversed numbers.]

COMPUTE RS ← $RI^2 + RJ^2 + RK^2$

Step 16. IF   R = RS

THEN PRINT I, J, K

END-IF

Step 17. COMPUTE K ← K + 1

Step 18. END-REPEAT K

Step 19. END-REPEAT J

Step 20. END-REPEAT I

Step 21. END

Problem 3.39. *Determine the difference between two given dates. Construct a flowchart to show how to do it.*

Task Analysis. The inputs required are the day, month, and year number of two dates. The difference between the dates can then be computed by comparing the day numbers first and then by taking the difference; the month numbers are then compared and the number of months in between is then obtained. Now, when the two day numbers are compared, the day number of the smaller date may be larger than that of the greater date. To obtain the number of days in the difference, we add 30 to the smaller day number and subtract 1 from the corresponding month number. Otherwise, the number of days in the difference can be obtained through outright subtraction. To obtain the number of months in the difference, we compare the month number in the larger date with that in the smaller date. If the month number in the larger date is smaller than that of the smaller date, then 12 is added to the corresponding month number and then the number of months in the difference can be obtained through subtraction. One is subtracted from the year number of the larger date. Otherwise, the number of months can be obtained through straightforward subtraction.

There will be no such problem in obtaining the number of years because the year in the larger date will always be larger than the year in the smaller date. The procedure is depicted below through flowchart.

The algorithm corresponding to Problem 3.39 is stated below:

Step 1. Set WISH to TRUE

Step 2. Repeat steps 3 to 12 WHILE WISH

Step 3. Accept the day (DD), month (MM), and year (YY) component of the larger date

Step 4. Accept the day (DD1), month (MM1), and year (YY1) component of the smaller date

Step 5. IF DD < DD1
  THEN COMPUTE DD ← DD + 30
    COMPUTE MM ← MM − 1
  END-IF

Step 6. COMPUTE D ← DD − DD1

Step 7. IF MM < MM1
  THEN COMPUTE MM ← MM + 12
    COMPUTE YY ← YY − 1
  END-IF

Step 8. COMPUTE M ← MM − MM1

Step 9. PRINT Y, "YEARS", M, "MONTHS", D, "DAYS"

Step 10. PRINT "CONTINUE? (Y/N)"

Step 11. INPUT TO CHOICE

Step 12. IF CHOICE ! = "Y"
  THEN Set WISH to FALSE
  END-IF

Step 13. END-WHILE

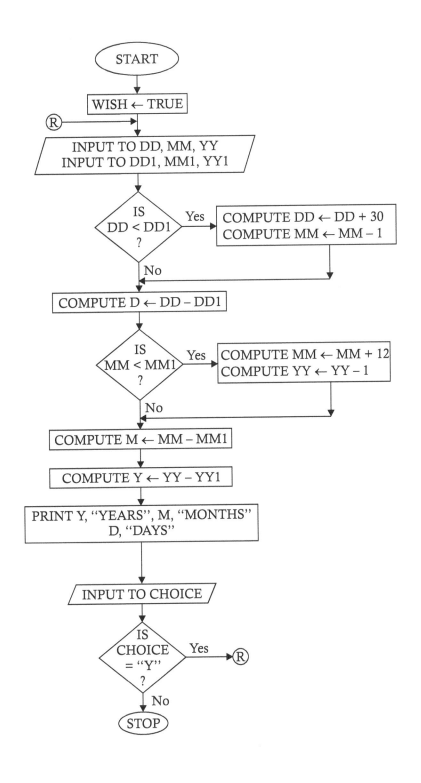

Problem 3.40. *Develop a flowchart to show how to find out all the groups of three successive numbers under 1000 that have the property that the square of the middle number is greater by unity than the product of the other two numbers (for example, $18^2 = 17 \times 19 + 1$).*

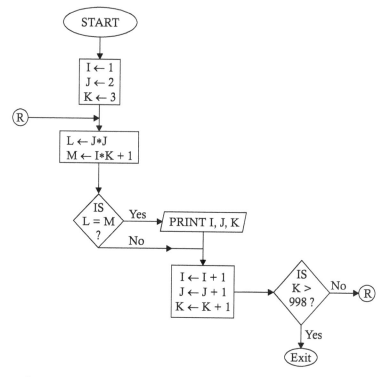

Task Analysis. We need to use the numbers up to 1000. As any set of three successive numbers can satisfy the requirement, we may start checking from the first three natural numbers, *i.e.*, 1, 2, and 3, and terminate the process when the largest of the numbers falls beyond 998. The procedure is as shown above.

The algorithm corresponding to Problem 3.40 is stated below:

Step 1. [INITIALIZE THREE VARIABLES FOR THE FIRST THREE NUMBERS]
$I \leftarrow 1$
$J \leftarrow 2$
$K \leftarrow 3$.

Step 2. REPEAT STEPS 3 TO 6 UNTIL K > 998

Step 3. [Obtain the square of the middle one]
COMPUTE $L \leftarrow J^2$

Step 4. COMPUTE M ← I*K + 1

Step 5. IF   L = M
          THEN PRINT I, J, K
          END-IF
Step 6. [INCREMENT EACH OF THE VARIABLES
          REPRESENTING THE NUMBERS]
              COMPUTE I ← I + 1
              COMPUTE J ← J + 1
              COMPUTE K ← K + 1
Step 7. END-REPEAT
Step 8. END

Problem 3.41. *Construct a flowchart to show how number of elapsed days between two dates.*

Task Analysis. The problem is to determine the difference between two dates in the number of days. For example, the number of days between July 12, 1985, and July 26, 1985, is 14. But in the determination of number of days between two dates that differ widely, say, February 10, 1969 and July 21, 1988, the calculation is a bit more complex. Luckily, there is a formula that can be used to calculate the number of days between two dates. This is affected by computing the value of N for each of the two dates and then by taking the difference, where N is calculated as follows:

$$N = 1461 \times f(\text{year, month})/4 + 153 \times g(\text{month})/5 + \text{days}$$

where

$f(\text{year, month})$ = year − 1, if month ≤ 2
              = year, otherwise
$g(\text{month})$ = month + 13, if month ≤ 2
              = month + 1, otherwise

and all calculations are performed using integer arithmetic.

As an example of applying the formula, to calculate the number of days between February 10, 1969 and July 21, 1988, we can calculate the values of N_1 and N_2 by substituting the appropriate values into the above formula as shown below.

$$N_1 = 1461 \times f(1969,2)/4 + 153 \times g(2)/5 + 10$$
$$= (1461 \times 1968)/4 + 153 \times (2 + 13)/5 + 10$$
$$= 2875248/4 + 2295/5 + 10$$
$$= 718812 + 459 + 10$$
$$= 719281$$
$$N_2 = 1461 \times f(1988,7)/4 + 153 \times g(7)/5 + 21$$
$$= (1461 \times 1988)/4 + (153 \times 8)/5 + 21$$
$$= 2904468/4 + 1224/5 + 21$$
$$= 726117 + 244 + 21$$
$$= 726382$$

The number of elapsed days = $N_2 - N_1$ = 719281 − 726382 = 7101.

The number of days between the two dates is 7101. The above formula is applicable for any date after March 1, 1900, (1 must be added to N for dates from March 1, 1800 to February 28, 1900, and 2 must be added for dates between March 1, 1700, and February 28, 1800, and so on). The steps of the solution are shown in the flowchart.

The algorithm corresponding to the solution of Problem 3.41 is described below:

Step 1. WISH = "Y"
Step 2. REPEAT Step 3 to Step 12 WHILE WISH = "Y"
Step 3. ACCEPT DATE 1, DATE 2
Step 4. [SEPARATE DAY, MONTH, AND YEAR]
DD1 ← Day Number of DATE 1
MM1 ← Month Number of DATE 1
YY1 ← Year Number of DATE 1
DD2 ← Day Number of DATE 2
MM2 ← Month Number of DATE 2
YY2 ← Year Number of DATE 2
Step 5. IF MM1 <= 2
THEN F1 ← YY1 − 1
G1 ← MM1 + 13
ELSE
F1 ← YY1
G1 ← MM1 + 1
END-IF
Step 6. IF MM2 <= 2
THEN F2 ← YY2 − 1
G2 ← MM2 + 13
ELSE
F2 ← YY2
G2 ← MM2 + 13
END-IF
Step 7. [COMPUTE N1] $N1 \leftarrow 1461 \cdot \dfrac{F1}{4} + 153 \cdot \dfrac{G1}{5} + DD$

Step 8. COMPUTE $N2 \leftarrow 1461 \cdot \dfrac{F2}{4} + 153 \cdot \dfrac{G2}{5} + DD$

Step 9. [CALCULATE THE NUMBER OF DAYS IN BETWEEN]
D ← N2 − N1
Step 10. PRINT D
Step 11. PRINT "WISH TO CONTINUE? (Y/N)"
Step 12. INPUT TO WISH
Step 13. END

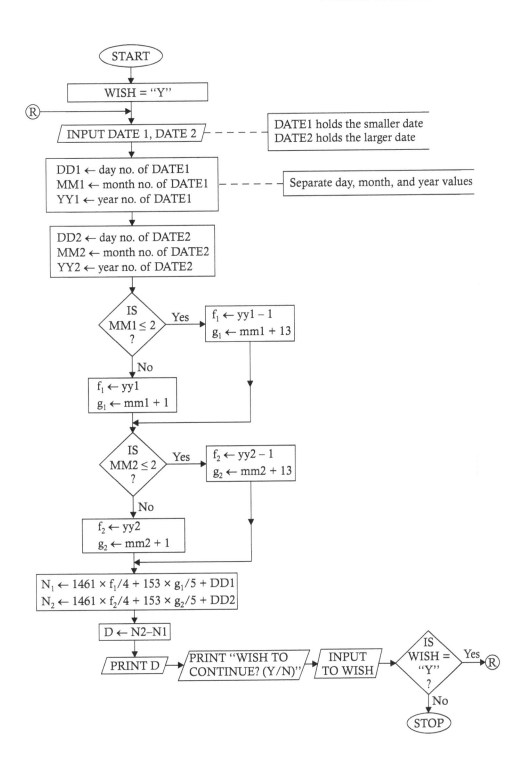

Problem 3.42. *Construct a flowchart to show how to determine the name of the starting day of any given year.*

Task Analysis. The name of a year can be determined on the basis of a day-code that varies from 0 to 6. The day-code value 0 implies "Sunday," day-code value 1 implies "Monday," and so on. The day-code of a year X can be determined by the following formula:

$$\text{day-code} = \left[X + \left[\frac{x-1}{4} \right] - \left[\frac{x-1}{100} \right] + \left[\frac{x-1}{400} \right] \right] \bmod 7$$

where [a] denotes the greatest integer less than or equal to *a*. For example [5.6] is 5. This is also known as floor value. Mod 7 implies remainder after division by 7.

The day-code value can also be computed by taking the value of N computed in the preceding problem and then subtracting 621,049 from it and then taking the result modulo 7. Here we use the previous procedure to construct the following flowchart because that is true for any year.

The algorithm corresponding to the solution of Problem 3.42 is stated below:

Step 1. REPEAT step 2 through step 10
Step 2. ACCEPT YEAR as input
Step 3. IF YEAR = 0
     THEN STOP
    END-IF
Step 4. COMPUTE Y1 ← Floor value of (Year − 1)/4
Step 5. COMPUTE Y2 ← Floor value of (Year − 1)/100
Step 6. COMPUTE Y3 ← Floor value of (Year − 1)/400
Step 7. COMPUTE V ← YEAR + Y1 − Y2 + Y3
Step 8. COMPUTE DAY-CODE ← REMAINDER OF (V/7)
Step 9. IF DAY-CODE = 0
    THEN DAY-NAME ← "SUNDAY"
    ELSE
      IF DAY-CODE = 1
        THEN DAY-NAME ← "MONDAY"
        ELSE IF DAY-CODE = 2
        THEN DAY-NAME ← "TUESDAY"
      ELSE IF DAY-CODE = 3
        THEN   DAY-NAME ← "WEDNESDAY"
        ELSE IF DAY-CODE = 4

THEN DAY-NAME ← "THURSDAY"
ELSE IF DAY-CODE = 5
    THEN DAY-NAME ← "FRIDAY"
        ELSE IF DAY-CODE = 6
            THEN DAY-NAME ← "SATURDAY"
        END-IF
    END-IF
    END-IF
END-IF
END-IF
END-IF
END-IF
Step 10. PRINT DAY-NAME
Step 11. STOP

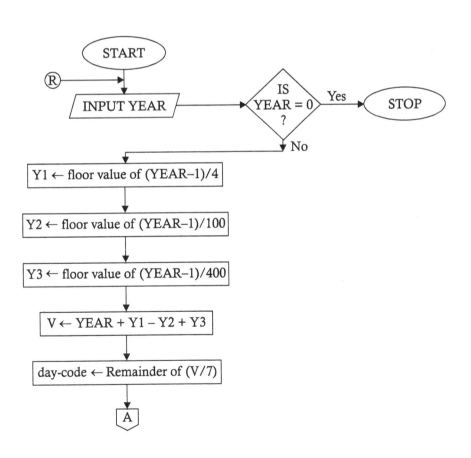

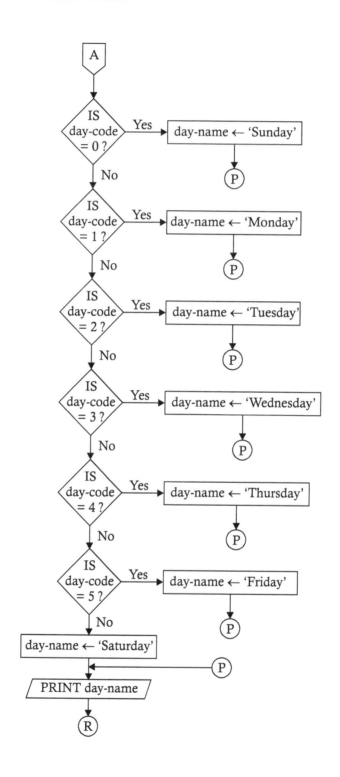

EXERCISES

Construct flowcharts to show the following:

(i) Print multiplication tables from 1 to 5

(ii) Sum the digits of a given number until it is reduced to a single digit

(iii) Create a pyramid of numbers consisting of a given number of lines. For example, if the given number is 5, then we should see the following:

$$
\begin{array}{ccccccccc}
 & & & & 1 & & & & \\
 & & & 1 & 2 & 1 & & & \\
 & & 1 & 2 & 3 & 2 & 1 & & \\
 & 1 & 2 & 3 & 4 & 3 & 2 & 1 & \\
1 & 2 & 3 & 4 & 5 & 4 & 3 & 2 & 1
\end{array}
$$

(iv) Sum the digits of a given number

(v) A menu of fruits as given below that accepts the user's option. Calculate the cost of fruits and repeat the same until the user's option is exited. Display the cost of each item and the total amount to be paid by the customer.

Fruits Menu

Fruits	Cost per Pound. (in $)
1. Mango	5.00
2. Apple	3.00
3. Grapes	2.00
4. Exit	

(vi) The following patterns with flexible dimensions as supplied by the uses:

(a)

(b)

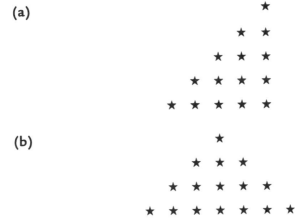

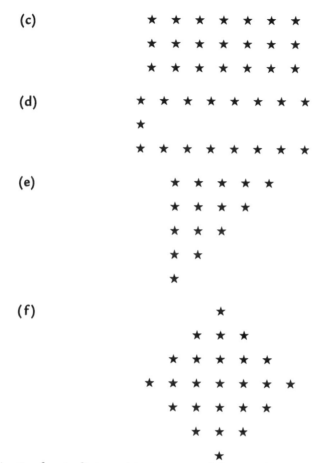

(vii) Read a six-digit positive integer. If the number is even, add up its digits. Otherwise, multiply the individual digits and print the result.

(viii) Obtain the decimal equivalent of a binary number

(ix) Display all characters represented by the ASCII numbers from 25 to 100

(x) Determine the value of an exponential expression of the form a^x, where a is any number and x is any integer

(xi) Determine the HCF of n given numbers

(xii) Determine the maximum and the minimum ones of n given numbers

(xiii) Determine all the permutations of the numbers less than or equal to some given number n.

For example, if $n = 123$, then the permutations are:

123

321

231

132

213

312

(xiv) Find a series of five consecutive numbers, the sum of the squares of the first three of which is equal to the sum of the squares of the last two. For example,

$$(-2)^2 + (-1)^2 + 0^2 = 1^2 + 2^2$$

(xv) Limit the checking within 1000, to show all the triad numbers within 10,000. A number is said to be a triad number if the double and triple of the number contain all separate digits with no repetition of any one of them.

(xvi) Identify and show the integer values of x, y, and z that satisfy the equation: $Z^2 = X^2 + y^2$

CHAPTER 4

PROBLEMS INVOLVING ARRAYS

INTRODUCTION

Think of a road with a row of houses on it. How would you get a unique address for a house on that road? You would take the name of the road and the house number of the lot. An array is similar to a road with a number of houses. The name of the road can be thought of as the name of the array and the number of the house can be thought of as the location number in the array.

Formally speaking, an array is a finite collection of homogeneous data values usually stored in consecutive memory locations with a common name. The term *finite* implies that the number of data values of an array must be limited by its size. The term *homogeneous* means "having the same nature or characteristic." The term *usually* implies that arrays are almost always implemented by using contiguous locations of the computer's main memory in a linearly ordered fashion, but not always. The common name assigned to a set of adjacent memory locations to hold the data of a particular type is called the *name* of the array. The different data values of an array are mentioned by using the name of the array along with a subscript within brackets, such as $A[1]$, $A(1)$, and $A[2]$, or in general, $A[i]$, where i must be an integer. The value of i is the location. The subscript is also called an *index*. This is why an array element such as $A[i]$ is also called an indexed or subscripted variable. The following are some examples of arrays:

1. The roll numbers of the students of a class stored in a computer's main memory in linear order

2. The names of the students of a class stored in the computer's main memory in linear order

3. The maximum temperatures of different days of a month in a city stored in the computer's memory in linear order

All of the data stored together are of the same type, *i.e.*, homogeneous. For example, roll numbers are usually integers, names are usually strings of characters, and temperatures are usually fractional or floating point numbers. Hence, the first example is an array of integers, the second example is an array of strings, and the third example is an array of floating point numbers. Different computer languages use different notations to represent the array elements. However, we will use just one notation. If A is an array of size n, then we will point to an array element by the notation A(i), where the value of i can vary from 1 to n.

Problem 4.1. *The goal here is to show you how to construct an array. The following algorithm will clarify the steps:*

1. Decide the size of the array to be formed, say n.

2. Declare an array of size n with some desired name, say A.

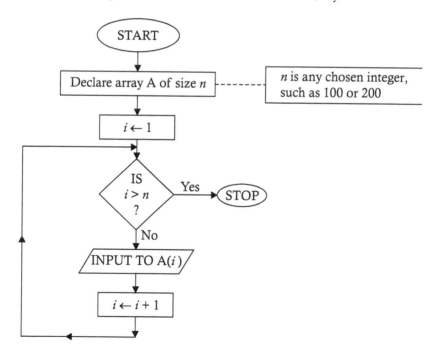

3. Initialize the variable or location that will be used as a subscript, say i, with a statement like $i \leftarrow 1$.

4. Repeat Steps 5 and 6 until $i > n$.

5. Accept the data value for the array element $A(i)$.

6. Increment the value of the subscript: $i \leftarrow i + 1$.

7. Stop.

In most of the programming languages, the first two Steps can be performed in a single statement where the size n is predefined, such as int A[100], which defines an array of integers of size 100.

However, mere construction of an array does not accomplish a goal. The stored values of an array need to be manipulated. The manipulation may be the simple viewing of the data stored or it may comprise some arithmetic or logical operations on the stored data.

Problem 4.2. *Let us define the objective of our array creation. We wish to view the stored data values in the reverse sequence of inputs, i.e., we want to see the last input value first and the first input value last and others in that sequence. With this purpose in mind, we re-write the above algorithm as follows:*

1. Decide the size of the array to be formed (n).

2. Declare an array of size n with some desired name (A).

3. Initialize the variable or location that will be used as a subscript, say i, with a statement like $i \leftarrow 1$.

4. Repeat Steps 5 and 6 while $i <= n$.

5. Accept the data value for the array element $A(i)$.

6. Increment the value of the subscript: $i \leftarrow i + 1$.

7. Set $i \leftarrow n$.

8. Repeat Steps 9 and 10 while $i >= 1$

9. Display $A(i)$

10. Set $i \leftarrow i - 1$.

11. Stop

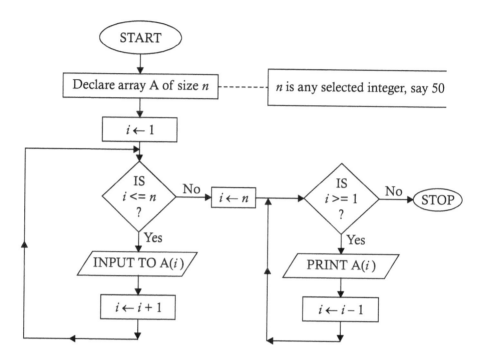

Problem 4.3. *Construct a flowchart to show how to rearrange the elements in an array so that they appear in reverse order.*

Task Analysis. The problem is to move the elements of an array from one place to another so that when the array is read sequentially from the beginning, we get the last element first, the second to last element as the second element, and so on. For example,

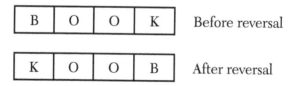

We can do this simply by exchanging the values of two locations taken at a time. We use two variables i and j. The value of i indicates the location on the left, starting from the first location, and that of j indicates the location on the right, starting from the last location. Now we can exchange the values of the ith and the jth locations of the array. After each exchange of values, we increase the value of i by 1 and decrease the value of j by 1 until $i > j$. Of course, the initial value of i should be 0—one less than the index of the first location, and that of j should be $n + 1$—one greater than the index of the last location.

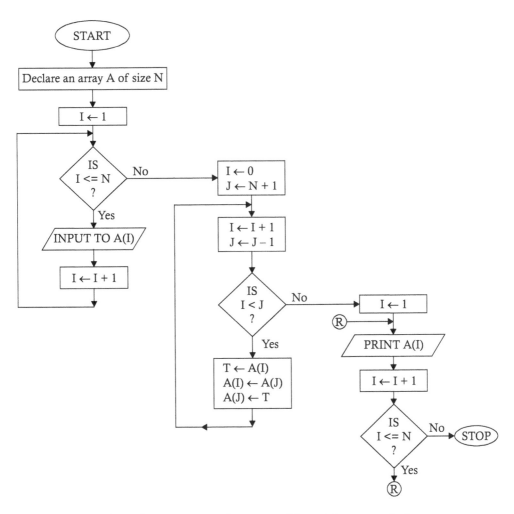

The algorithm corresponding to Problem 4.3 is given below:

Step 1. Declare the array A(1 ... N) of N elements to be reversed.
Step 2. Repeat Step 3 for I = 1 to N.
Step 3. Accept a data value at the Ith location.
Step 4. Set I = 0, J = N + 1
Step 5. Repeat steps 6 through 7 until I >= J
Step 6. I ← I + 1, J = J – 1
Step 7. T ← A (I)
A(I) ← A(J)
A(J) ← T

Step 8. Repeat step 9 for I = 1 to N
Step 9. PRINT A(I)
Step 10. STOP

Problem 4.4. *Construct a flowchart to show how to determine the maximum number in a set of n numbers.*

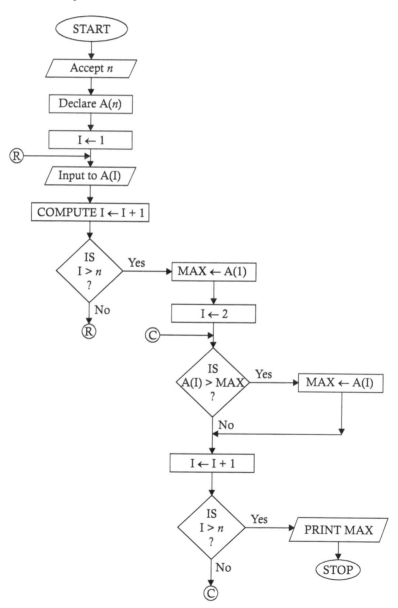

Task Analysis. The maximum number in a set of numbers is that number which is greater than or equal to all other numbers in the set. The maximum number may not be unique and it is only defined for sets of one or more elements. The simplest, most systematic way to find the desired number is achieved if we consider the first number as our temporary candidate for the maximum and write it in a separate place, MAX. Then we scan the list from the 2nd number through the last number of the list to find any number that is greater than the number stored in MAX. If we find such a number, we store it in MAX by removing the previously stored one. At the end of the scanning process, we can declare that MAX contains the largest number in the given set. The algorithm of the solution is given here.

Step 1. Accept the size of the set, n.
Step 2. Declare an array A(1 ... n) of n elements where $n \geq 1$.
Step 3. Repeat step 4 for I = 1, 2, ..., n.
Step 4. Accept a number to A(I).
Step 5. [Set temporary maximum MAX to first array element] MAX ←A(1).
Step 6. Repeat step 7 for I = 2, 3, ..., n.
Step 7. If A(I) > MAX,
   Then MAX ← A(I)
   End-if
Step 8. Print MAX as the maximum for the array of n elements.
Step 9. Stop.

Problem 4.5. *Construct a flowchart to show how to store the first 100 natural numbers in an array and then show them in the reverse sequence.*

Task Analysis. To solve the problem, we need an array of dimension 100. The array can be filled with natural numbers automatically and once stored, the numbers can be returned by pointing to the locations, starting from the last location. The solution is shown in the flowchart of Problem 4.5.

The algorithm corresponding to Problem 4.5. is given below:

Step 1. Declare an array of size 100 with any chosen name, say A.
Step 2. Initialize the variable that will be used as a subscript, say I, with a statement like I ← 1
Step 3. REPEAT steps 5 and 6 UNTIL I > 100.
Step 4. A(I) ← I
Step 5. I ← I + 1
Step 6. Initialize I again with the starting print location, I ← 100
Step 7. REPEAT STEPS 9 & 10 UNTIL I < 1.

Step 8. PRINT A(I).
Step 9. I ← I – 1
Step 10. END.

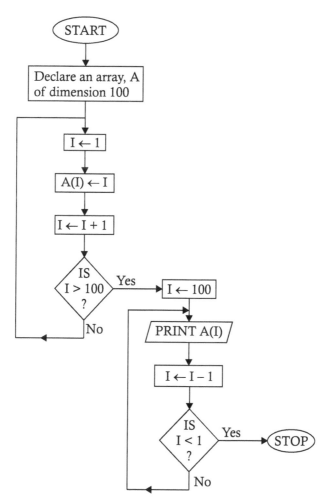

Problem 4.6. *In a certain hospital, the weights of newborn babies are recorded each month and then processed at the end of the month to determine the following:*

   (i) *mean weight of the babies*

  (ii) *maximum of the weights*

 (iii) *minimum of the weights*

Construct a flowchart to show how the weights can be stored in the computer's memory first and then processed to determine the desired outputs.

Task Analysis. The solution includes the procedure for storing the weights of the babies first. This requires an array. Let us suppose that the dimension of the array can be given as the input during the execution of the procedure, so that the array can be defined during the execution. (If it is not possible, then an array of size 100 may be defined and then the requisite number of locations can be used.) The next task is to determine the maximum of the weights recorded. We assume that the weight stored in the first location is the maximum one, and hence we store its value to some location, say MAX. Next, we compare the values of the remaining locations one by one with the value of the MAX; if it happens that some location contains a weight greater than that of the MAX, then we store that weight in MAX by removing the previous one so that at the end of the comparison, the location MAX will contain the maximum of the weights. Similarly, the minimum of the weights can be determined by defining a location, say MIN, with the initial value of the first location and then comparing the value of MIN with the values of the remaining locations to find the value lesser then the value contained in MIN.

The algorithm corresponding to Problem 4.6 is given below:

Step 1. ACCEPT THE SIZE(N) OF THE ARRAY AS INPUT

Step 2. DECLARE AN ARRAY W OF SIZE N.

Step 3. I ← 1 [INITIALIZE THE VARIABLE I WITH 1 FOR USE AS A SUBSCRIPT]

Step 4. REPEAT STEPS 5 and 6 WHILE I < = N

Step 5. INPUT TO W(I) [W(I) is to hold the weight of Ith baby given as input]

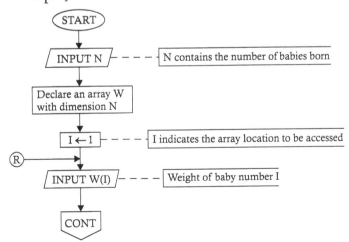

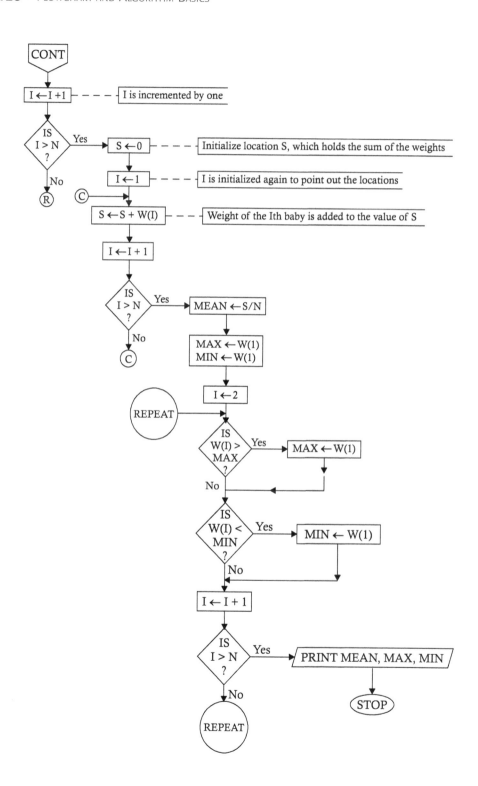

Step 6. COMPUTE I ← I + 1 [INCREMENT I]
Step 7. S ← 0 [INITIALIZE S, which is the sum of the weights of the babies]
Step 8. I ← 1
Step 9. REPEAT STEPS 10 and 11 WHILE I <= N
Step 10. COMPUTE S ← S + W(I)
Step 11. COMPUTE I ← I + 1
Step 12. COMPUTE MEAN ← $\dfrac{S}{N}$
Step 13. MAX ← W(1) [Initialize MAX with the weight of the 1st baby]
Step 14. MIN ← W(1) [Initialize MIN with the weight of the 1st baby]
Step 15. I ← 2 [Set I to 2, to start comparison with the weight of the 2nd baby onwards]
Step 16. REPEAT STEPS 17 THROUGH 19 WHILE I <= N
Step 17. IF W(I) > MAX
　　　　　THEN MAX ← W(I)
　　　　　END-IF
Step 18. IF W(I) < MIN
　　　　　THEN MIN ← W(I)
　　　　　END-IF
Step 19. COMPUTE I ← I + 1
Step 20. PRINT MEAN, MAX, MIN
Step 21. STOP

Problem 4.7. *In a certain city, the maximum and the minimum temperatures on each day are recorded each month to determine the following at the end of the month:*

 (i) *mean maximum temperature in the month*

 (ii) *mean minimum temperature in the month*

(iii) *highest maximum temperature*

(iv) *lowest minimum temperature*

 (v) *hottest day number of the month*

(vi) *coldest day number of the month*

　　Draw a flowchart to show how the desired result can be obtained.

Task Analysis. This problem is similar to the preceding one. Hence, the solution will also be similar. Two arrays are required to store the two types of data (maximum and minimum). The output includes two more things: the hottest day number and the coldest day number of the month. These day numbers of the hottest day and that of the coldest day are stored in two variables named "HOTTEST" and "COLDEST," respectively.

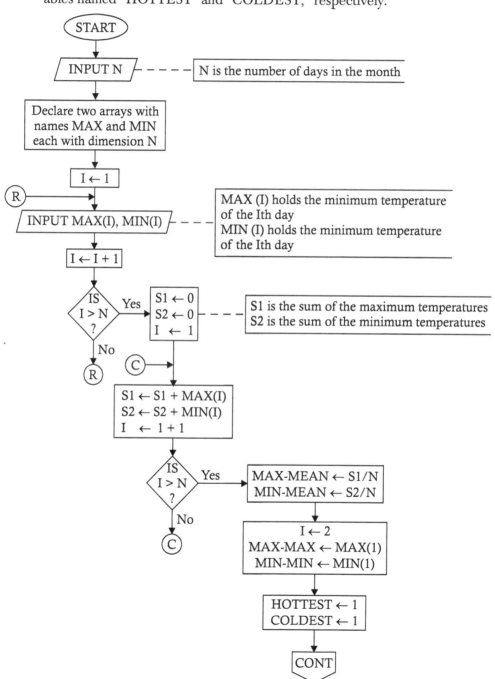

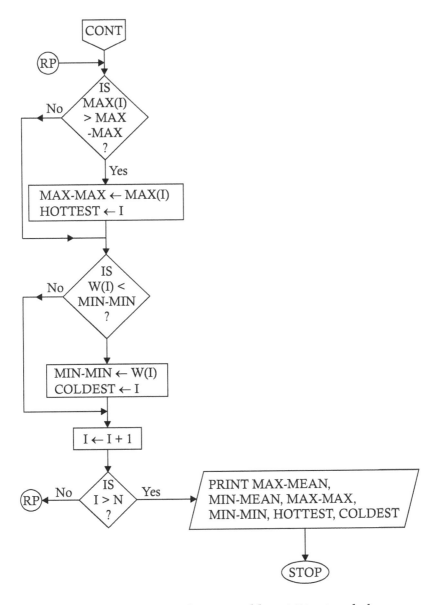

The algorithm corresponding to Problem 4.7 is given below:

Step 1. ACCEPT SIZE N OF THE ARRAY AS INPUT
Step 2. DECLARE TWO ARRAYS WITH NAMES MAX and MIN
Step 3. REPEAT FOR I = 1, 2, 3, ..., N
    (*a*) INPUT TO MAX (I)
    (*b*) INPUT TO MIN (I)

Step 4. S1 ← 0, S2 ← 0
[Initialize S1 and S2, which are the sum of maximum and minimum temperatures, respectively]

Step 5. REPEAT FOR I = 1, 2, 3, ..., N
(a) COMPUTE S1 ← S1 + MAX (I)
(b) COMPUTE S2 ← S2 + MIN(I)

Step 6. COMPUTE MAX-MEAN ← $\dfrac{S1}{N}$

Step 7. COMPUTE MIN-MEAN ← $\dfrac{S2}{N}$

Step 8. MAX-MAX ← MAX (1) [Initialize with the 1st temperature of the set]

Step 9. MIN-MIN ← MIN (1) [Initialize with the 1st temperature of the minimum set]

Step 10. HOTTEST ← 1, COLDEST ← 1
[Initialize with the 1st day number]

Step 11. REPEAT FOR I = 2, 3, 4, ..., N
IF MAX (I) > MAX-MAX
THEN MAX-MAX ← MAX (I)
HOTTEST ← I
END-IF
IF MIN (I) < MIN-MIN
THEN MIN-MIN ← MIN (I)
COLDEST ← I
END-IF

Step 12. PRINT MAX-MEAN, MIN-MEAN, MAX-MAX, MIN-MIN, HOTTEST, AND COLDEST

Step 13. END

Problem 4.8. *Three tests are given, each one worth 50 points. The better score of the first two tests is added to that of the third one to determine the final score and a grade is assigned to each student on the percentage score as per the following rules.*

Percentage in Score	Grade
> = 80	A
> = 70 but <80	B
> = 60 but <70	C
> = 50 but <60	D
< 50	F

Develop a flowchart to show how to accept the input data related to each student and process them to print out a result sheet with the output in descending order of the percentage score.

Task Analysis. The inputs are the grades obtained by students on three tests. To identify the student, the student roll-number and name of each student are given as input. The final score of each student is obtained by determining the greater score of the first two tests and then adding it to that of the third test. The total score represents the percentage score because the total is based on the marks of two tests, each of which carries a maximum grade of 50.

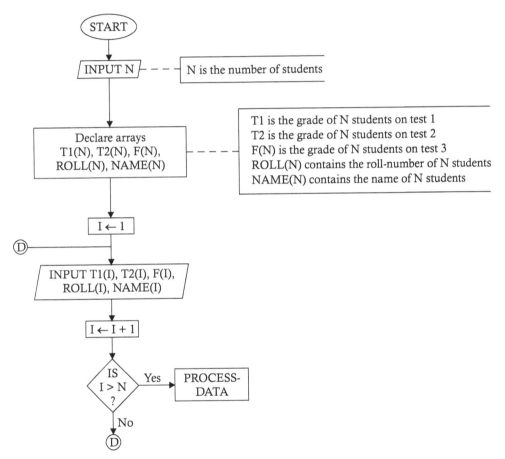

At this stage, we shall have the Roll Number, Name, and Percentage of all the students. The next task is to sort the facts to get information about the students in a descending sequence of percentages. To sort the facts, we take the percentage of the first student and compare it with the percentage of all the other remaining students and interchange the student's data whenever some student's percentage is found to be less than the percentage of that of the first student's percentage. Similarly, we take the percentage of the second student to compare it with the percentage of the third student to interchange the facts, if needed. This type of comparison is continued until we compare the percentage of the last two students.

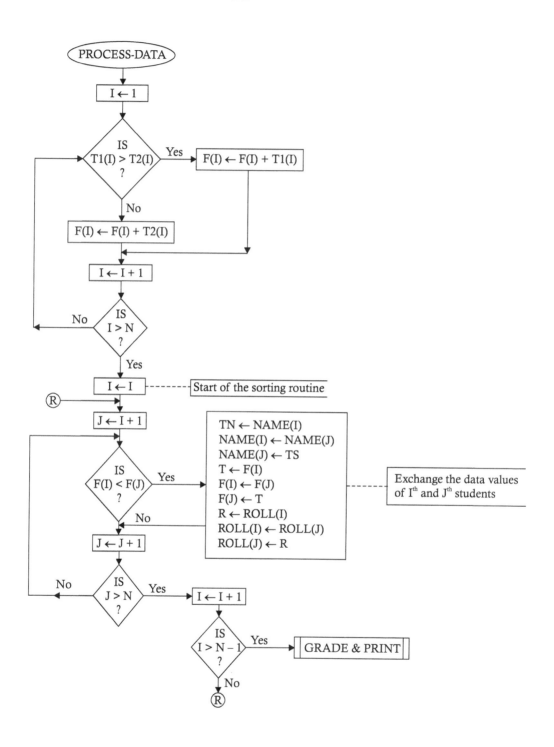

During the interchange operations, the roll-number and the name of the students must also be interchanged.

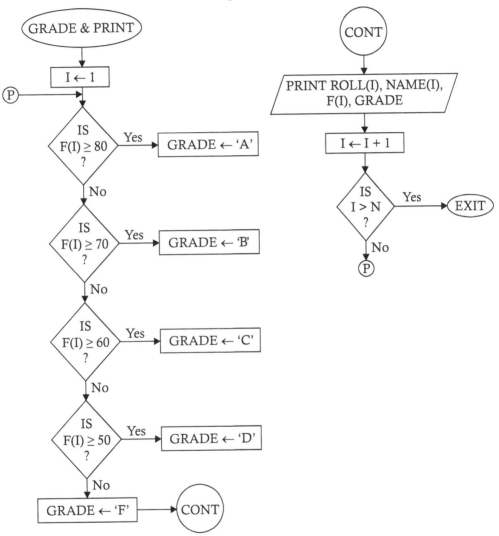

The algorithm of Problem 4.8 is shown below:

Step 1. ACCEPT THE NUMBER OF STUDENTS N
Step 2. DECLARE FIVE ARRAYS: T1(I), T2(I), F(I), ROLL (I), AND NAME (I) TO HOLD THE SCORES OF TEST 1, TEST 2, TEST 3, THE ROLL NUMBER, AND NAME OF THE STUDENTS, RESPECTIVELY.

Step 3. I ← 1 [INITIALIZE I]
Step 4. REPEAT STEP 5 AND STEP 6 WHILE I <= N
Step 5. INPUT TO T1(I), T2(I), F(I), ROLL (I), NAME (I)
Step 6. COMPUTE I ← I + 1
Step 7. I ← I
Step 8. DO STEP 9 and STEP 10 WHILE I <= N
Step 9. IF T1 (I) > T2 (I)
      THEN COMPUTE F(I) ← F(I) + T1(I)
   ELSE
      COMPUTE F(I) ← F(I) + T2 (I)
   END-IF
Step 10. COMPUTE I ← I + 1
Step 11. I ← 1
Step 12. REPEAT STEP 13 THROUGH STEP 15 WHILE I <= N – 1
Step 13. COMPUTE J ← I + 1
Step 14. FOR J = I + 1 TO N DO
   IF F(I) < F(J)
      THEN T ← F(I)
         F(I) ← F(J)
         F(J) ← T
         R ← ROLL (I)
         ROLL (I) ← ROLL (J)
         ROLL (J) ← R
         TN ← NAME (I)
         NAME (I) ← NAME (J)
         NAME (J) ← TN
   END-IF
Step 15. COMPUTE I ← I + 1
Step 16. FOR I = 1, 2, 3, ..., N DO
   (*i*) IF F (I) ← 80
      THEN GRADE ← 'A'
      ELSE IF F(I) ←70
        THEN GRADE ← 'B'
      ELSE IF F(I) ← 60
        THEN GRADE ← 'C'
      ELSE IF F(I) ←50
        THEN GRADE ← 'D'
      ELSE
        GRADE ← 'F'

        END-IF
        END-IF
        END-IF
        END-IF
        (*ii*) PRINT F(I), ROLL (I), NAME (I), GRADE
Step 17. STOP

Problem 4.9. *Construct a flowchart to show how a set of N numbers is stored in memory and then stored in ascending order of their magnitude for display.*

Task Analysis. Let us suppose that the list of numbers A(1), A(2), ..., A(N) is in the memory. We use a bubble sort algorithm that works as follows:

Step 1. We compare A(1) and A(2) and arrange them in the desired order, so that A(1) < A(2). We next compare A(2) and A(3) so that A(2) < A(3). We continue this way until we compare A(N – 1) with A(N) and arrange them so that A(N – 1) < A(N). These comparisons bring the largest element to the Nth position, *i.e.*, the largest of the elements comes in A(N) after these N – 1 comparisons.

Step 2. As the largest element has been placed properly in Step 1, we need not disturb the A(N) element. We repeat the comparisons in Step 1 without A(N). This will bring up the second largest element in A(N – 1).

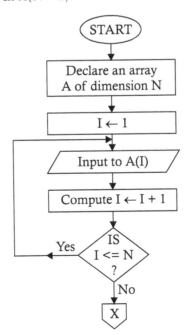

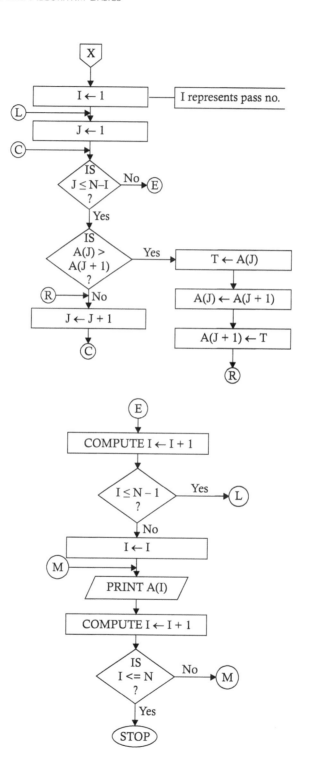

We repeat these comparisons each time, considering one less element than that in the preceding step. It can be observed that after (N – 1) steps, the set of numbers will be in the sorted sequence.

The algorithm of the above process is stated below:

Step 1. FOR I = 1 TO N
Step 2. INPUT TO A(I)
Step 3. END-FOR
Step 4. FOR I = 1 TO N – 1
Step 5. FOR J = 1 TO N – I
Step 6. IF A(J) > A(J + 1)
THEN T ← A(J)
A(J) ← A(J + 1)
A(J + 1) ← T
END-IF
Step 7. END-FOR–J
Step 8. END-FOR–I
Step 9. FOR I = 1 TO N
Step 10. PRINT A(I)
Step 11. END-FOR–I
Step 12. STOP

Problem 4.10. *Draw a flowchart to show how the product of two matrices can be obtained.*

Task Analysis. We know that a matrix is a two-dimensional array. The multiplication of two matrices is possible if the number of columns of the first matrix is equal to the number of rows in the second matrix or if the number of rows in the first matrix equals the number of columns of the second matrix. If we consider the row-by-column multiplication of the two matrices, then each element of a row is taken sequentially to multiply with the corresponding column elements, taking one at a time, and the sum of these products is taken as an element of the resulting matrix. This is repeated for all the rows of the first matrix. The reverse process is carried out for the column by row multiplication. To describe the process mathematically, let $A = [a_{ij}]$ be an $m \times n$ matrix and $B = [b_{ij}]$ be an $n \times p$ matrix. Then the product A.B of these matrices is of the order $m \times p$ say, $C = [c_{ij}]$.
where $c_{ij} = a_{i1} \cdot b_{1j} + a_{i2} \cdot b_{2i} + \ldots\ldots + a_{in} \cdot b_{nj}$

$$\Rightarrow \qquad\qquad c_{ij} = \sum_{k=1}^{n} a_{ik} \cdot b_{kj}$$

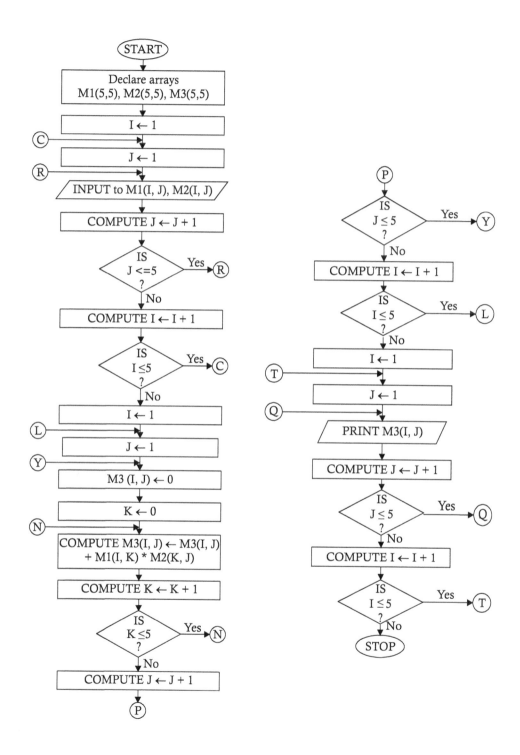

The algorithm of Problem 4.10 is given below:

Step 1. FOR I = 1 TO 5
Step 2. FOR J = 1 TO 5
Step 3. Input TO M1(I, J), M2 (I, J)
Step 4. NEXT J
Step 5. NEXT I
Step 6. FOR I = 1 TO 5
Step 7. FOR J = 1 TO 5
Step 8. M 3 (I, J) = 0
Step 9. FOR K = 1 TO 5
Step 10. COMPUTE M3 (I, J) ←M3(I, J) + M1(I, K) * M2(K, J)
Step 11. END-FOR-K
Step 12. END-FOR-J
Step 13. END-FOR-I
Step 14. FOR I = 1 TO 5
Step 15. FOR J = 1 TO 5
Step 16. PRINT M3 (I, J)
Step 17. END-FOR-J
Step 18. END-FOR-I
Step 19. STOP

Problem 4.11. *A departmental store chain consists of 15 stores, each comprising 7 departments. The weekly sales totals of each department of the stores are available for processing.*

Develop a flowchart to show how the data are to be processed to determine the total Weekly Sales.

(i) *Department* **(ii)** *Store*

Task Analysis. We need three arrays: one two-dimensional array to hold the sales values and two one-dimensional arrays, one to hold the department totals and one to hold the store averages. The procedure involves the row-wise addition of two-dimensional array values when the total for each store is determined and column-wise addition of the two-dimensional array-values when the total for each department is determined.

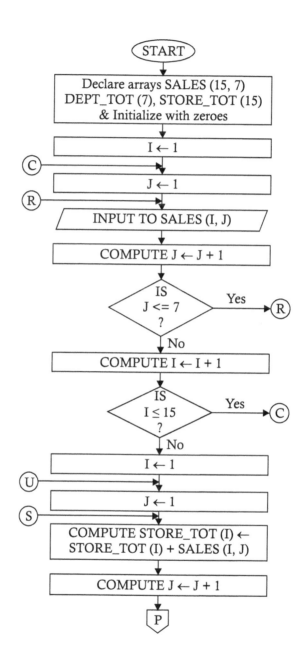

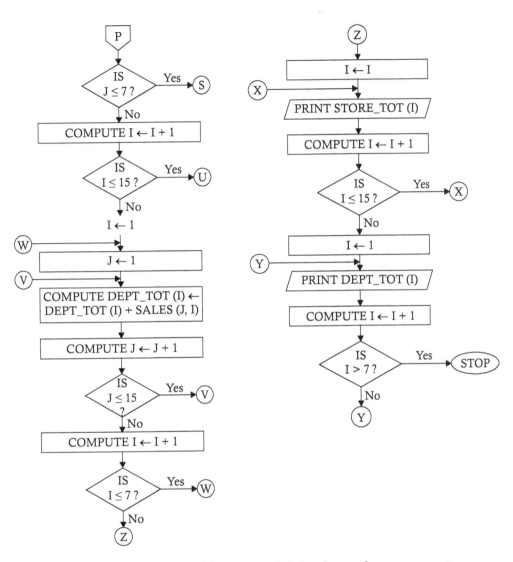

The algorithm of Problem 4.11 is left for the reader as an exercise.

EXERCISES

Construct flowcharts and algorithms for the following problems:

1. Convert a decimal number into its equivalent binary, octal, or hexadecimal form according to the given option.

2. Test whether a given string is a palindrome.

3. Count the number of vowels, consonants, and special characters in a given string.

4. Unscramble a four-letter word.
   [**Hint.** Let abcd be the given four-character string. The process should find out all the words by jumbling the characters, such as acbd and adbc.]

5. Convert a given Roman numeral into its decimal equivalent. The following table gives the Roman numerals and their decimal equivalents:

Roman	Decimal
M	1000
D	500
C	100
L	50
X	10
V	5
I	1

The algorithm for converting a Roman numeral

$$R1, R2, ...Rn$$

to a decimal is given below:

1. $I \leftarrow 1$
   (I denotes the position of the symbol being scanned)
2. DECIMAL $\leftarrow 0$
   DECIMAL is to hold the decimal value of the given Roman numeral)
3. REPEAT steps 4 through 6 WHILE $I < N$.
4. If the decimal value of R_i is greater than or equal to the decimal value of R_{i+1}, add the decimal value of R_i to DECIMAL else subtract the decimal value of R_i from DECIMAL.
5. COMPUTE $I \leftarrow I + 1$.
6. END-WHILE.

7. ADD the decimal value of R_n to DECIMAL.
8. PRINT DECIMAL.
9. STOP.

6. Convert a decimal number into its Roman equivalent.

7. Show that Goldback's conjecture in mathematics is true for all the positive even numbers under 500.
(Goldback stated that every even integer greater than 2 can be expressed as the sum of two prime numbers.)

8. The maximum and the minimum temperatures on each day of a city are collected over each month and then processed to determine

   (i) average minimum temperature of the month
   (ii) average maximum temperature of the month
   (iii) lowest temperature during the month and the day number on which it occurred
   (iv) highest temperature during the month and the day number of the month on which it occurred

9. Obtain the sum and the difference of two matrices.

10. A fishing fleet fishes in 10 different regions each consisting of 8 different areas. The data about the fish caught in kilograms are available for processing. Determine

    (i) region-wide average amount of fish caught
    (ii) area-wide average amount of fish caught
    (iii) the area of the region that yielded the highest catch
    (iv) the area of the region that yielded the lowest catch
    (v) grand total of the fish caught

Show the data in a tabular format.

CHAPTER 5

THE ART OF FILE PROCESSING

INTRODUCTION

A *file* may generally be defined as an organized collection of well-ordered, well-related, and self-contained information held on a stable storage medium. The information in a file is placed in a specific way and read back in a specific way. The information must be kept together as a unit in the same sequence in a well-organized way. The different units of information must bear some relationship with one another for collective consideration. A file is self-contained in that it is complete in all respects. The stable storage medium may be a piece of paper, a magnetic or optical disk, or a magnetic tape or any other medium where the information can be kept for a long time for repeated use without any special aid. Thus, the information bearing the characteristics mentioned above stored in the main memory of a computer will not make a file because the main memory of a computer can hold it only as long as electricity is supplied to the main memory.

Depending on the nature of the information, files can be classified into two basic types: the program file and the data file. A *program file* is a file that contains a sequential set of instructions in a computer language that can direct a computer in the performance of some specific task. A *data file* is a collection of records about closely-related or similar entities. However, these types of files should possess all the features stated in the generalized definition above. A *record* is an ordered collection of the attribute values of an entity. An *attribute* is any characteristic or feature of an entity that tells something about the entity, where an entity is anything with a physical or conceptual existence. A *fact* is anything that is true about an entity. To collect facts about an entity, we first decide on some attributes of the entity and procure facts on those attributes. We normally choose a group of entities called an *entity set*, a collection of items that are considered together for some close relationship. We next select some of the attributes common to all the entities of the set and collect facts on those attributes in a predefined order to form a record for each of them and put all such records together to form the desired file. Let us consider a business enterprise, for instance. The employees of the enterprise form a closely related set of entities. If we consider the attributes EMPLOYEE-CODE-NUMBER, EMPLOYEE-NAME, EMPLOYEE-ADDRESS, DESIGNATION, and SALARY for each of the employees, then the values of these attributes in the mentioned order form a record of an employee of the enterprise and the collection of all the records of the employees of the enterprise forms the desired employee data file (if the records are kept on a stable storage medium).

A file is typically considered a data file. The task of file processing is the set of activities performed on the records of a file to generate some desired information. Now depending on the organization of the records, the set of operations will vary. We next consider a discussion on file organization. Basically, file organization can be classified into three categories:

(i) Sequential File Organization
(ii) Indexed File Organization
(iii) Hashed/Relative/Random File Organization

Sequential file organization is one in which records are kept in a file, one after another, and processed in the same sequence in which they are written. The term sequential means one after another, and hence the name bears the nature of the organization of the file.

Indexed file organization is one in which sequentially organized records are associated with an index for the purpose of direct access to the records. An *index* is a special kind of file that contains records consisting of two attribute values, one that is a unique identifying attribute of the records in the sequential file and the other that contains the address of the records in the main file. The identifying attribute is also known as the *key attribute* or *key field*. The records in the index are kept in the ascending order of the key field values. When a user wishes to access a record from an indexed file, she initiates a binary search in the index for some key field value and the record found in the search process is then accessed to get the address of the desired record in the main file. Thus, any record in an indexed file can be accessed without reading the preceding or the following records in the file. This saves time and increases the speed of processing, if the number of records to be accessed in one processing run is less than one-fourth of the total number of records in the file. The disadvantage of such a file organization is that it takes additional disk space for the index, and hence the file organization is more expensive than sequential file organization. The speed of accessing records also varies depending on the organization of the records in the index. For more details about the index file organization, please see any standard textbook on databases or file management systems.

A hashed or relative file organization is also a direct access file organization. In such a file organization, the key field or identifying attribute value is hashed or converted to some location address in the file space relative to the beginning of the file-record positions on the basis of some predefined function. The predefined function is called a *hash routine* and the method is called *hashing*. As the hashing is done dynamically during the creation of the file, no extra file space is needed for this purpose, rather, the records can be pointed to directly later by using the same hash function. The only problem with this type of organization is the proper selection of the hash function and its implementation through programming instructions. The programming efficiency of the developers is considered when selecting one of the two direct access file organizations. (The reader is again advised to read a textbook on file/database management systems for further details.) We now study different problems on file processing to illustrate the flowcharts and the algorithms corresponding to their solutions. The following problems involve sequential file organization.

Problem 5.1. *Construct a flowchart to show how the records of the students in a computer training institution are kept in a file. Each record consists of*

- **(i)** STUDENT-ID (for unique identification of the students)
- **(ii)** STUDENT-NAME
- **(iii)** COURSE-NAME
- **(iv)** COURSE-FEE
- **(v)** FEES-PAID
- **(vi)** DATE-OF-ADMISSION

Task Analysis. The logic of this problem is straightforward. Data is accepted from the terminal for the attributes for one student at a time in the order of their specification to form a student record and then the record is written in the file space designated through the opening statement of a file until the user signals there are no more records to be written in the file. The file space is then delinked by writing a statement for closing the file. The user's signal for no more records to be written in the file can be indicated by inputting an invalid data value for the first attribute of the record, say 0 for STUDENT-ID.

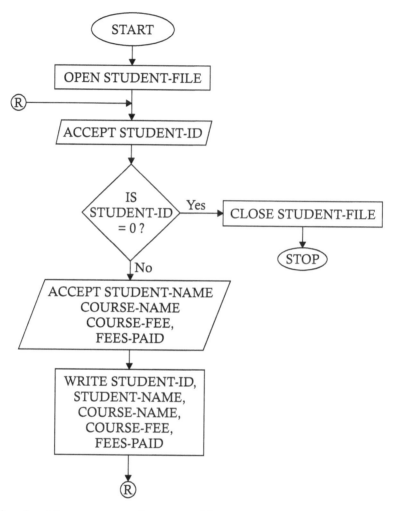

The algorithm corresponding to Problem 5.1 is as follows:

Step 1. OPEN STUDENT-FILE
Step 2. REPEAT STEPS 3 THROUGH 7
Step 3. ACCEPT STUDENT-ID
Step 4. IF STUDENT-ID = 0
     THEN
      (*i*) CLOSE STUDENT-FILE
      (*ii*) EXIT
     END-IF
Step 5. ACCEPT STUDENT-NAME, COURSE-NAME, COURSE-FEE, FEES-PAID

Step 6. WRITE STUDENT-RECORD

Step 7. END

Problem 5.2. *Develop a flowchart to process the records of the STUDENT-FILE mentioned in Problem 5.1 to create another file containing records of the students having dues where each record will consist of STUDENT-ID, STUDENT-NAME, and DUE-AMOUNT.*

Task Analysis. Two files must be used here. The first file, STUDENT-FILE, contains the input records that are to be read one by one, and the second file, DUES-FILE, contains the records of the students with dues. The student with dues can be found if we see that fees paid by the student are less than the course fee. The due amount can then be obtained by subtracting the fees paid from the course fee of the student. This gives us the data values of the records to be written in the output file named DUES-FILE. The process is terminated as soon as we reach the end of STUDENT-FILE. We check the end of a file against a logical value EOF. The EOF is defined in a variety of ways in different programming languages.

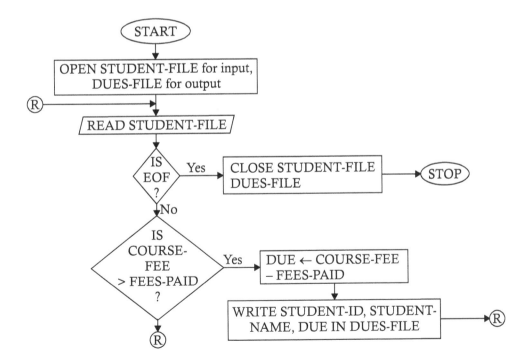

The algorithm corresponding to Problem 5.2 is shown below:

Step 1. OPEN INPUT STUDENT-FILE, OUTPUT DUES-FILE
Step 2. REPEAT STEPS 3 THROUGH 5
Step 3. READ A RECORD FROM STUDENT-FILE
Step 4. IF EOF OF STUDENT-FILE
    THEN
      (*i*) CLOSE STUDENT-FILE
      (*ii*) EXIT
    END-IF
Step 5. IF COURSE-FEE > FEES-PAID
    THEN DUE ← COURSE-FEE – FEES-PAID
    WRITE STUDENT-ID, STUDENT-NAME, DUE
    IN DUES-FILE
    END-IF
Step 6. STOP
Step 7. END

Problem 5.3. *A file named EMPFL contains the records of the employees of an organization. Each record consists of data: EMP-CODE, EMP-NAME, and BASIC-PAY. The gross salary of an employee is calculated by using the following formula: Gross Salary = Basic Pay + DA + ADA + HRA + MA*

where   *DA = 45% of Basic Pay*
          ADA = 18% of Basic Pay subject to a minimum of $200 and
               a maximum of $1000.
          HRA = 25% of Basic Pay subject to a minimum of $500 and
               a maximum of $5000.
          MA = 10% of the Basic pay subject to a minimum of $100.
The net salary of an employee is calculated by the formula:
          Net Salary = Gross Salary – Total Deduction
where   *Total Deduction = PF + PT*
where   *PF = 12% of Basic Pay*
          PT = 5% of Basic Pay subject to a maximum of $200.

Develop a flowchart and the algorithm to show how the salary for different employees is calculated to generate the pay slips for the employees of the organization.

Task Analysis. The problem here is to print the pay slip for each of the employees whose records are contained in EMPFL. This can be done by reading the records of the employees one at a time and then calculating the

DA, ADA, HRA, and MA values to determine the gross salary and then finding out the amounts of PF and PT for determining the total deduction. The net salary can then be obtained by subtracting the total deduction from the gross salary. The ADA is 18% of Basic Pay, subject to a minimum of $200 and a maximum of $1,000. This implies that if the 18% of the Basic Pay value happens to be less than $200, then $200 is the ADA amount; if, however, it exceeds $1,000, then $1,000 is the ADA amount. The conditions for HRA, MA, and PT can be handled in the same way.

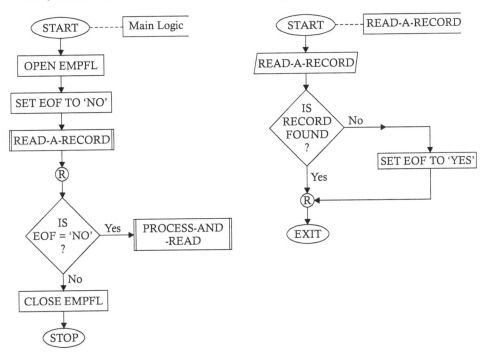

Note that the flowchart has three modules: Main Logic, READ-A-RECORD, and PROCESS-AND-READ. The flowchart of the last two modules is shown separately. In a programming language, these can be implemented as distinct procedures or functions. The algorithm of Problem 5.3 is shown below:

Step 1. OPEN EMPFL
Step 2. REPEAT STEPS 3 THROUGH 18
Step 3. READ A RECORD
Step 4. IF EOF IS TRUE
          THEN (*i*) CLOSE EMPFL
             (*ii*) EXIT

```
            END-IF
Step 5.     COMPUTE DA ← BASIC-PAY * .45
Step 6.     COMPUTE ADA ← BASIC-PAY *.18
Step 7.     IF ADA > 1000
                THEN ADA ← 1000
            ELSE
            IF ADA < 200
                THEN ADA ← 200
            END-IF
            END-IF
Step 8.     COMPUTE HRA ← BASIC-PAY * .25
Step 9.     IF HRA < 500
                THEN HRA ← 5000
            ELSE
            IF HRA > 5000
                THEN HRA ← 5000
            END-IF
            END-IF
Step 10.    COMPUTE MA ← BASIC-PAY * .10
Step 11.    IF MA < 100
                THEN MA ← 100
            END-IF
Step 12.    COMPUTE PF ← BASIC-PAY * .12
Step 13.    COMPUTE PT ← BASIC PAY * .05
Step 14.    IF PT > 200
                THEN PT ← 200
            END-IF
Step 15.    COMPUTE  GROSS-PAY ← BASIC-PAY + DA + ADA +
            HRA + MA
Step 16.    COMPUTE TD ← PF + PT
Step 17.    COMPUTE NET-PAY ← GROSS-PAY – TD
Step 18.    PRINT EMPCODE,
            EMPNAME,
            GROSS-PAY, TD,
            NET-PAY
Step 19.    STOP
```

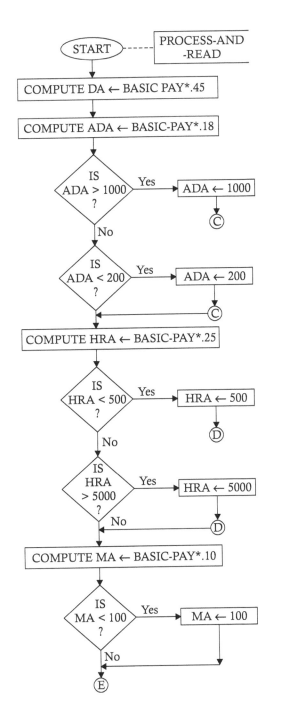

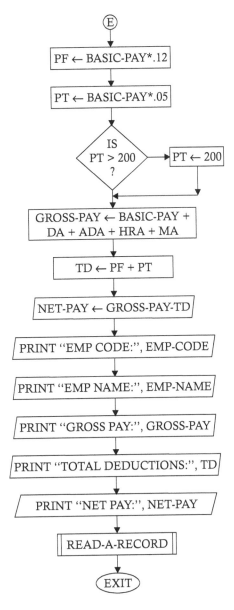

Problem 5.4. *A file named INVENT contains records of assets in the inventory of a company for the computation and printing of the depreciation schedule for each of them. Each record consists of the ASSET-MEMBER, ASSET-VALUE, RATE, and YEARS, where RATE contains the rate of depreciation and YEARS contains the life-span of the asset over which the asset will be depreciated. The following table illustrates the desired form of the output for an asset.*

Asset	45678	Original Value $1,000.00	Rate 0.20
Year	Depreciation	Accumulated Depreciation	Book Value
1	$200.00	$200.00	$800.00
2	160.00	360.00	640.00
3	128.00	488.00	512.00
4	102.40	590.00	409.00
5	89.92	672.32	327.68

Construct a flowchart to show the processing logic of the problem. Develop the algorithm of the solution.

Task Analysis. Depreciation is the monetary value by which the value of some asset is reduced for each year of use. The calculation of depreciation is straightforward here. The asset-value and the rate by which the asset-value is to be reduced are both given in each record. We read each record and then multiply the asset-value by the rate to obtain its current value of depreciation. When an item is depreciated, its asset-value decreases, so to compute the next year's depreciation, the depreciation amount is subtracted from the current asset-value to obtain its current face value (or *book value*). This calculation is repeated to print the depreciation schedule of an asset over its life span. HEADER-1 is the first line of text, along with values from the record read, as shown in the illustration. The HEADER-2 is the second line of text, as illustrated.

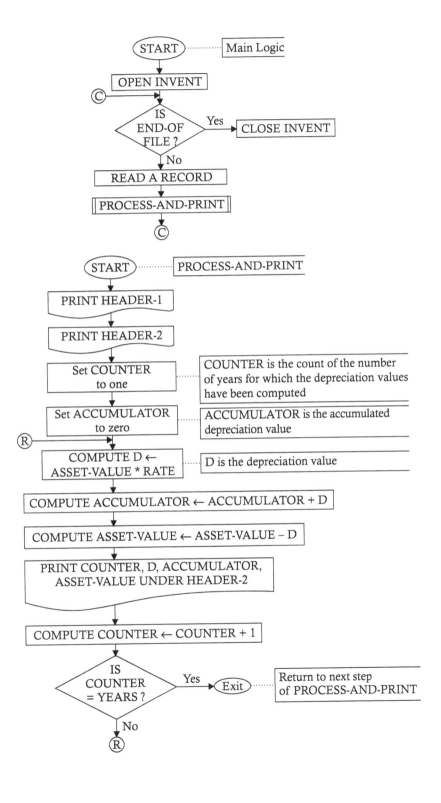

The algorithm of Problem 5.4 is given below:

Step 1. OPEN INVENT FILE
Step 2. REPEAT STEPS 3 THROUGH 14 WHILE NOT END OF FILE
Step 3. READ A RECORD
Step 4. PRINT ASSET-NUMBER, ORIGINAL-VALUE, RATE WITH text as HEADER-1
Step 5. PRINT "YEAR," "DEPRECIATION," "ACCUMULATED DEPRECIATION" and "BOOK VALUE" as column headings
Step 6. SET COUNTER TO 1
Step 7. SET ACCUMULATOR TO 0
Step 8. REPEAT STEPS 9 THRU 13 UNTIL COUNTER-YEARS
Step 9. COMPUTE D ← ASSET-VALUE * RATE
Step 10. COMPUTE ACCUMULATOR ← ACCUMULATOR + D
Step 11. COMPUTE ASSET-VALUE ← ASSET-VALUE – D
Step 12. PRINT COUNTER, D, ACCUMULATOR, ASSET-VALUE under column headings
Step 13. COMPUTE COUNTER ← COUNTER + 1
Step 14. END-WHILE
Step 15. CLOSE INVENT FILE
Step 16. END

Problem 5.5. *A sorted data file named RECEIVABLES contains records about the accounts-receivable of a company. Construct a flowchart to show how to generate a summary of the overdue and forthcoming receivables. Assume that each record consists of ACCOUNT-NO, YEAR-DUE, DAY-DUE, and AMOUNT-DUE.*

Task Analysis. The datafile must be sorted in the ascending order of the ACCOUNT-NO. We may assume that there is only one record per account. To print the desired output, the current (today's) date and year should be accepted from the terminal or from the system. The sample output for this problem is shown in the table.

Account Out of Sequence 005367		
Status	Number of Accounts	Value (in $)
Overdue	05	10,000.00
Receivable	03	5,000.00
Totals	02	15,000.00

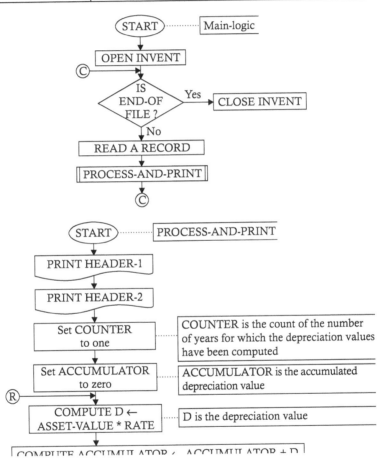

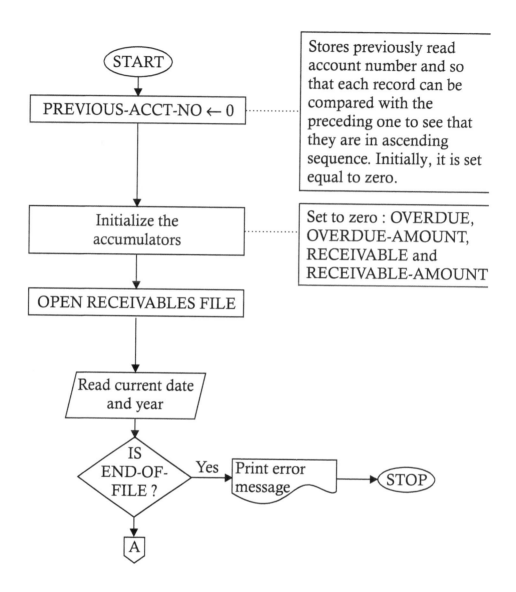

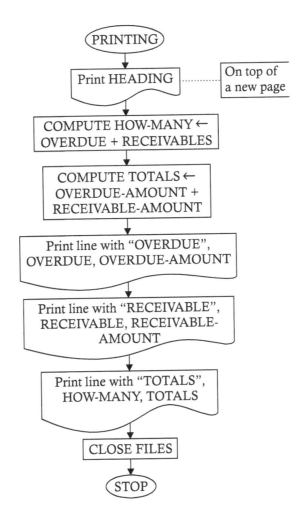

Problem 5.6. *In India, the registration charge for letters is calculated as per the following rules:*

For the first 20 grams (or part thereof), the charge is fixed and it is equal to Rs. 8.25 for domestic letters and Rs. 25.75 for international letters.

For the every additional 15 grams (or part thereof), the charge is Rs. 7.25 for domestic letters and Rs. 18.25 for international letters, as long as the gross weight does not exceed 500 grams.

For weights above 500 grams, the charge is calculated at the rate Rs. 1.65 per gram for domestic letters and at the rate of Rs. 4.65 per gram for international letters.

Develop a flowchart for the following:

(i) *Accept weight and type of letter interactively to calculate the charge and display it;*

(ii) *If the sender agrees to register the letter at the calculated charge, add a record to a register file consisting of the letter number, destination, weight, charge, date of registration, and letter type, and then print out a receipt for the sender in the following format:*

Receipt of Registration (Not Insured)
Letter No.:
Destination:
Weight:
Charge:
Date:

Signature

Task Analysis. The logic of this program is simple. A file named LNO-FILE contains an initial letter number. The subsequent letter numbers are obtained by incrementing this letter number. Another file named LETTER-FILE is kept open and contains the records of the registered letters sequentially. Each record of LETTER-FILE consists of a unique letter number, destination, weight, charge, date of registration, and type of letter in the order mentioned. The input data required from the terminal are the weight and type of letter on the basis of the weight and the type of letter. The registration charge can be computed according to the rules. The calculated charge can then be displayed for the confirmation of the sender. If the sender wishes to pay the calculated charge to get the letter registered, then a receipt of registration is printed in the given format and a record is appended to the open file.

In the flowchart, the computation of the 15-gram intervals is done using the following formula:

$$INV = \text{integer part of } \frac{(\text{ExcessWeight} - 1)}{15} + 1$$

The reader can check the validity of the formula for any additional weight. The algorithm of Problem 5.6 is stated below:

Step 1. OPEN LNO-FILE, LETTER-FILE
Step 2. REPEAT STEP 3 THROUGH 15
Step 3. ACCEPT W from the terminal [W is the weight of the letter to be registered]

Step 4. IF W <= 0 THEN EXIT

Step 5. ACCEPT LT from the terminal [LT is the type of letter (domestic or international)]

Step 6. IF W <= 20

THEN IF LT = "I"

THEN CHG ← 8.25

ELSE IF LT = "F"

THEN CHG ← 25.75

ELSE

PRINT "INVALID LETTER TYPE"

GO TO STEP 5

END-IF

END-IF

ELSE IF W <= 500

THEN COMPUTE EW ← W − 500

$$\text{COMPUTE INV} \leftarrow \text{INT}\left(\frac{EW-1}{15}\right)+1$$

IF LT = "I"

THEN COMPUTE CHG ← 8.25 + INV * 7.25

ELSE IF LT = "F"

THEN COMPUTE CHG ← 25.75 + INV * 18.25

ELSE PRINT "INVALID LETTER TYPE"

GO TO STEP 5

END-IF

END-IF

ELSE IF LT = "I"

THEN COMPUTE CHG ← 8.25 + 32 * 7.25 + (W − 500) * 1.65

ELSE IF LT = "F"

THEN COMPUTE CHG ← 18.75 + 32 * 18.25 + (W − 500) * 4.65

ELSE PRINT "INVALID LETTER TYPE" GO TO STEP 5

END-IF

END-IF

END-IF

Step 7. DISPLAY CHG

Step 8. ACCEPT RESPONSE

(TO DETERMINE WHETHER THE SENDER WISHES TO REGISTER THE LETTER AT THE CALCULATED CHARGE)

Step 9.   IF RESPONSE = "N"
THEN GO TO STEP 3
END-IF
Step 10. ACCEPT DESTINATION from the terminal
Step 11. READ LNO from LNO-FILE
Step 12. COMPUTE LNO ← LNO + 1
(Generate new LNO)
Step 13. PRINT RECEIPT
Step 14. WRITE a record in LETTER-FILE
Step 15. END-REPEAT
Step 16. END

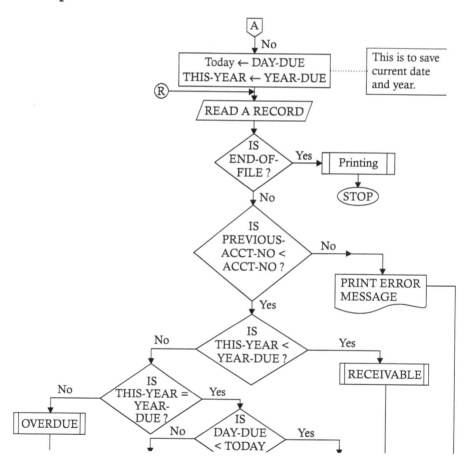

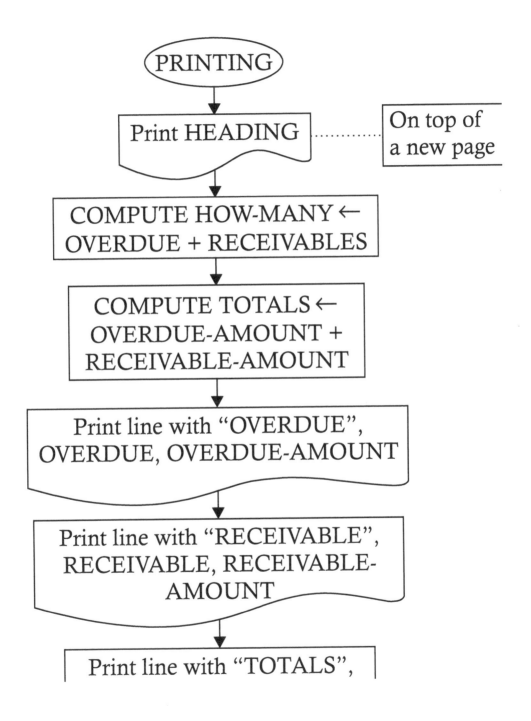

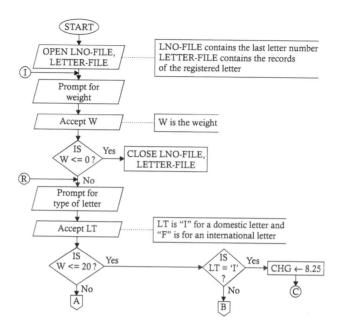

Problem 5.7. *ABC university conducted an examination and collected the students' personal data and the total points obtained in the examination in a file named STUDENTS. The record layout is given below:*

Data Description	Data Type & Size
Roll Number	*5 numeric*
Name of the Student	*25 alphabetic*
Sex Code (M: Male F: Female)	*1 alphabetic*
Marital Status Code (U: Unmarried; M: Married, D: Divorced; W: Widowed)	*1 alphabetic*
Age in Years	*2 numeric*
Total Points Obtained	*3 numeric*

The university authorities require the students' results in printed form to have the following information for each student:

1. Roll Number

2. Title of the Student (MR/MISS/MRS.)

3. Name of the Student

4. Age in Years

5. Total Marks Obtained

6. Result (PASSED/FAILED)

7. Grade (EXCELLENT/VERY GOOD/ GOOD/ FAIR/POOR)

At the end of the results of all the students, the following summary should be provided.

Summarized Information

| Sex | Passed | | | | | Failed | Total No. of Students |
	Excellent	V. Good	Good	Fair	Total	Poor	
No. of Girls							
No. of Boys							

The following criteria were adopted to provide the grades of the students:

Marks Obtained	Result	Grade
≥ 900	Passed	Excellent
< 900 but ≥750	Passed	Very Good
< 750 but ≥ 500	Passed	Good
< 500 but ≤ 400	Passed	Fair
< 400	Failed	Poor

The criteria for generating the title of each student is as follows:

1. If the sex code is "M," then the title is "MR."

2. If the sex code is "F," and the marital status is "U," then the title is "MISS."

3. If the sex code is "F," and the marital status is "M" or "D" or "W," then the title is "MRS."

Construct a flowchart to show the processing logic of the STUDENTS file to get the information desired. Show the algorithm of the solution.

Task Analysis. The problem consists of two major activities, namely, (*i*) developing the result, grade, and the title of each student for the given data, and printing the information in the desired format; and (*ii*) obtaining the summary totals to be printed at the end of the process.

The title of a student is generated from the combination of the sex code and the marital status code, as per the criteria stated in the problem statement. The result and the grade of the student are developed from the points obtained, as per the criteria stated. Depending upon the sex code and the grade, the summary controls are developed. Lastly, the required information is printed.

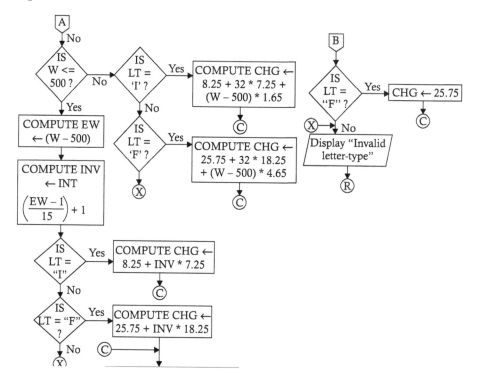

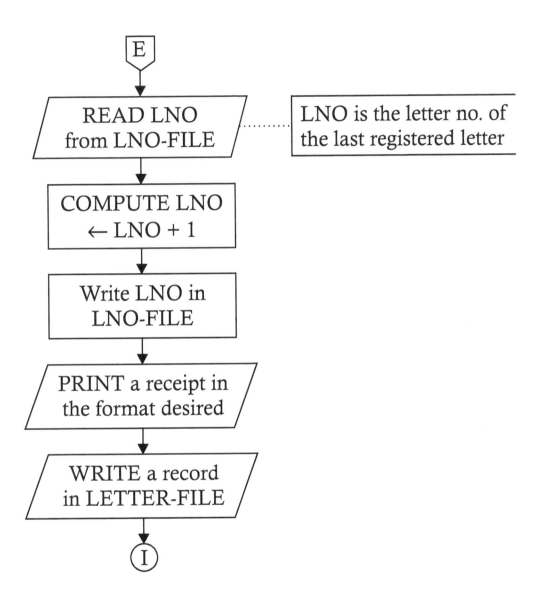

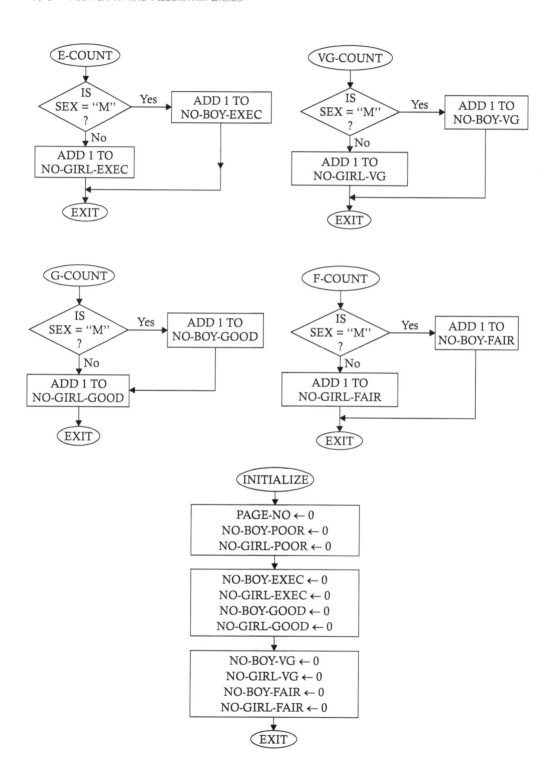

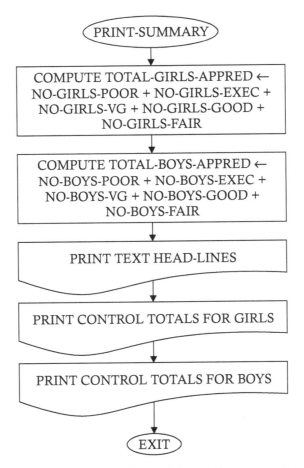

The algorithm of the solution for Problem 5.7 is summarized below:

Step 1. OPEN the input file STUDENTS

Step 2. Initialize PAGE-NO and the 10 counters for the summary information

Step 3. PRINT the page heading

Step 4. WHILE NOT END OF FILE REPEAT STEP 5 THROUGH STEP 9

Step 5. GENERATE the title as per the sex and the marital status code

Step 6. Depending upon the points obtained, generate the grade and the result of the student. Depending upon the sex code and the grade of the student the record is counted in one of the 10 counters for the summary.

Step 7. PRINT a student-record
Step 8. ADD 1 TO Line-counter
Step 9. IF Line-counter > 50
THEN PRINT page-heading in the next page
END-IF
Step 10. CALCULATE total for 'BOYS'
Step 11. CALCULATE total for 'GIRLS'
Step 12. PRINT total for 'BOYS'
Step 13. PRINT total for 'GIRLS'
Step 14. CLOSE STUDENT file
Step 15. STOP

Problem 5.8. *A branch of a nationalized bank (ABC Bank) has computerized the savings accounts of its consumers. As a result, they provide a monthly statement to customers stating their transactions every month.*

The data related to the name and address of the customer, bank account number, and opening balance for every month are kept in a disk file called SBMAST.DAT. This file is sorted in the order of account number. All the transactions for the customers are entered in another file called SBTRAN. DAT. At the end of every month, the transaction file is sorted using the account number and matched with the Master file for the printing out detailed statement for each customer.

The format of the two input files is given below:

SBMAST-DAT

Data Name	Description	Type & Size
BR-CODE	Branch Code	4 AN
SB-ACT-NO	Account Number	10 AN
NAME	Name of Customer	25 AN
ADDR	Address	30 AN
OPENING BALANCE	Opening balance at the beginning of month	$N(7 + 2)$

Savings Bank Transaction File: SBTRAN.DAT

Data Name	Description	Type & Size
SB-ACT-NO	Account Number	10 AN
TR-DAT	Transaction Date	8 AN
DESCRN	Description	15 AN

DEBIT	Withdrawals	(6 + 2) N
CREDIT	Deposits	(6 + 2) N

The name and address of the customer are printed as taken from the Master file. The account number is printed on the top right-hand side. The closing balance of the account is the opening balance credit/debit. Please note the following, which will help to write the correct algorithm.

There is one record in the Master file for each customer. In the transaction file, there may be no records (for a customer who has not had any transactions during the month) or there may be multiple records, if a customer has more than one transaction during the month. In the case of accounts with no transactions, the opening balance and closing balance and closing balance (both would be the same) are printed on consecutive lines. The remarks column contains the message "NO TRANSACTIONS" on the closing balance line. For all customers who have had transactions, every transaction is printed as a separate line, the opening balance being the first line. The opening balance line contains the words "OPENING BALANCE" in the description column of the line. The last line contains the final closing balance, with the words "OPENING BALANCE'" in the description column of the line. The last line contains the final closing balance, with the words "Closing Balance" in the description column. No dates are printed on the opening balance lines.

The data printed on the report for each transaction are in the DD-MM-YY format. The transactions are printed double-spaced, with 30 lines per page. There is a page skipped after every customer transaction is printed. The page number is initialized after every customer transaction is printed. The month and year of statement are taken from the terminal at a beginning of the program.

Normally, there should be no instance of the closing balance becoming negative for any customer. If however, the closing balance becomes negative, the balance should be printed with a negative sign, and the error message "NEGATIVE BALANCE" should be printed in the remarks column.

In the case of a customer who has only transactions, but no corresponding record in the Master file, the records should be bypassed, with the following message on the terminal: "NO MASTER FOR S/B ACCOUNT NO." The account number should be displayed by the side.

Use only the standard file-names for the input, and output and the data-names as specific above, in the input files. In the case of print record and other intermediate values that may be required, use the following standard names:

Print Record:	SBPRT-REC	
Data Names:	RPT-DATE	Data of Transaction
	RPT-EES	Description of Transaction
	RPT-OB	Opening Balance
	RPT-CR	Credit
	RPT-DR	Debit
	RPT-CB	Closing Balance
	REMK	Remarks

Other Data Names: CUMBAL Cumulative balance, starting from the opening balance to which credits are added and debits are subtracted to arrive at the closing balance

MSG1	"OPENING BALANCE"
MSG2	"CLOSING BALANCE"
MSG3	"NO TRANSACTIONS"
MSG4	"BALANCE NEGATIVE"
MSG5	"NO MASTER FOR S/B ACCOUNT NO:"
PG	Page Number
MY	Month and Year accepted from terminal

In case it becomes necessary to use any other data name other than what have been given above, a comment statement explaining what the data name stands for should be given.

Draw a flowchart showing the processing logic. Write comment statements to explain the processing logic.

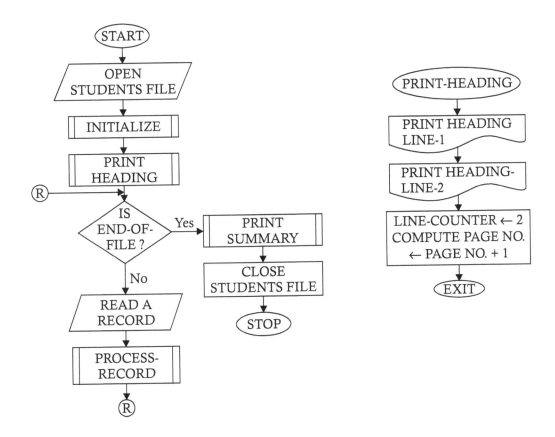

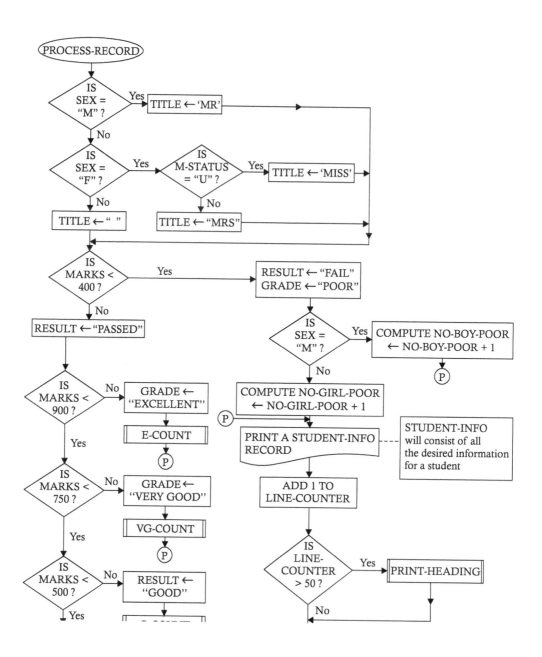

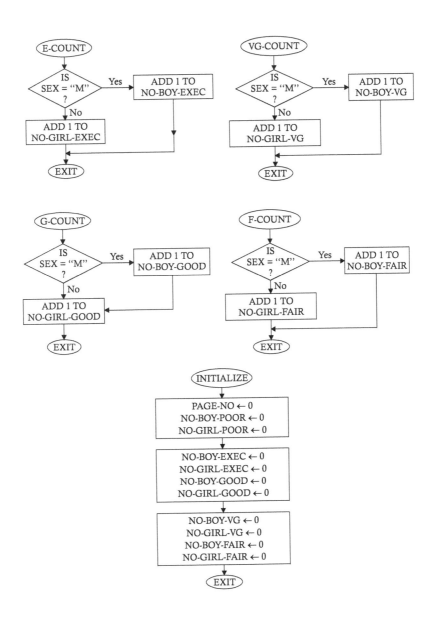

INDEXED FILE ORGANIZATION

An indexed file is a direct access file, and hence it is created only on a disk. This type of file organization allows for the sequential storage of records but facilitates random accessing or processing. An indexed file consists of two principal components: the main file and the index. The main file contains records in sequential order. The index or index file contains records consisting of two fields: the first field is the key field and the second field is the address field that holds the address of the physical location of the record in the main file. The records in the index are kept in the ascending sequence of the key field values of the records. A particular type of an indexed file is IBM's Indexed Sequential Access Method (ISAM) file. It uses an index file consisting of two levels: the cylinder index and the track index. A search method utilizes the index tables to determine the approximate storage location for a given record and then the desired record can be accessed through a scanning process.

Some programming languages, such as COBOL, possess features for the creation and maintenance of an indexed file. Popular programming languages, such as C and C++, do not possess such features. In C and C++, the index files can be organized through coding. As there is no standard universal way of using indexed files, this approach is not included here.

RELATIVE FILE ORGANIZATION

A relative file is also a direct access file that consists of records identified by a key that contains information about the location of a record in the file. In an indexed file, the identifier key has to be looked up in the table to determine the location of a record in the file. In contrast, record keys in a relative file contain information about the locations of records. This information is the relative address of a record. A record's relative address is its position in the file (first, second, third, and so on). Once we have the relative address, we can quickly determine approximately where the record is located in the file and then access it directly. A relative file is thus analogous to an array. Just as each of the array's elements has a position relative to the first, so it is for each element in a relative file that has a position relative to the first. A relative key value is obtained from the identifier field in a record, *i.e.,* the record key through some key-to-address transformation routine. Such a routine is called a *hash function* (this is why it is also called a *hashed file organization*). As the records can be accessed randomly approximately within the same interval of time by using the hashed value, called a *relative key*, a relative file is also called a *random file*. There are many different ways to define hash functions. The most popular one is the division remainder method.

Here, we define the hash function h by the rule

$$h \text{ (key)} = \text{key } \% \text{ divisor}$$

where the symbol % is the modulo operator that gives the remainder after dividing the record key by divisor. The divisor selected is the largest prime number less than the maximum file size defined. Normally, the file size is increased by 25% from what is actually required. Problems arise when two distinct record keys hash to the same relative storage address. Such a phenomenon is called a *collision* and the address for which the collision occurs is called a *synonym*. The file size is increased by 25% to reduce the chance of collisions. Any hashing system must provide a collision resolution policy (a way of handling collisions). We can use a collision resolution policy known as linear probing. When a collision occurs, we scan the following record locations until we find the first vacant location and store the record there (with the first record position is assumed to follow the last record position). When retrieving a record, we retrieve the record in the original location; if it is not the one we want, we keep searching in succeeding locations until we get the record identified by its key.

EXERCISES

(i) Draw a flowchart to show how SALESFILE is created by accepting data from the terminal for each record. The record consists of the code number of a salesperson, name of the person, and sales amount in a month. Write the algorithm of the solution.

(ii) Consider SALESFILE from in problem 1. Construct a flowchart showing how a sales report is generated in the format outlined below:

SALES REPORT OF XYZ LTD.
FOR THE MONTH OF DECEMBER 2019

SALES PERSON CODE	NAME	SALES-AMOUNT	COMMISSION
IOL001	SWAPAN SEN	10,000	3,500
		⋮	⋮
		⋮	⋮
	GRAND TOTALS:	...	...
NET SALES:		...	...
AVERAGE NET SALES:		...	...
AVERAGE COMMISSION:		...	

The rules for calculating the commission are as follows:

SALES	RATE
<= 5000	2% of SALES
> 5,000 but <=20,000	3.5% of SALES
> 20,000 but <= 50,000	5% + $1,000
> 50,000	7% + $2,500

Develop the algorithm of the solution.

(iii) A company maintains inventory data in a file named ITEMFL. The master file is stored on part number and contains the following types of data for each item held in the inventory.

Field	Data Type and Size
Part number	5 numeric positions
Part name	15 alphanumeric positions
Quantity in stock	5 numeric positions

Another data file named TRANSFL contains the records of transactions on the items in the inventory. Each record of this file consists of the following:

Field	Data Type and Size
Part number	5 numeric positions
Transaction code 1 = receipt 2 = issue	1 numeric position
Quantity transacted	5 numeric positions.

Draw a flowchart to show how the master file is updated on the basis of the records of the transaction file. Develop an algorithm for the solution of the above problem.

(iv) A data file contains invoice records. The layout of the records is given below:

Field	Data Type and Size
Party Code	5 alphanumeric
Invoice Number	6 Numeric
Invoice Data	6 (DD MM YY)
Gross =Value	$7 & cents
Discount Amount	$6 & cents
Sales Tax Amount	$7 & cents
Net Payable	$7 & cents

The records have been kept sorted in ascending sequence of the Invoice Number.

Accumulate the totals of the Gross Value, Discount, Sales Tax, and Net Payable amounts, and print the totals. Draw a flowchart showing the processing logic and write the algorithm of the solution.

(v) A credit bureau maintains a master file that lists for, each of its customers, a unique identification number, name, current principal that the customer owes, and his or her credit limit. The credit bureau also maintains a transaction file that tracks its customers' loans and payments. Each record in this file lists the customer's identification number, together with the transaction's amount and its date. A positive number indicates a payment and a negative number indicates a loan. Once a month, the credit bureau updates its master file by processing entries in the transaction file. Assume that the master file records are sorted by identification number, but the transaction file is not sorted.

Construct a flowchart and then develop the algorithm showing the program logic to update the master file.

INDEX